BRANDEE JANKOSKI

Easy Eats For Teens

Over 100 Delicious Recipes for Teens to Master!

First edition

Contents

4.   Lunch Time

5. Appetizers and Snacks

6. Dinner Mains

7.   On the Side

8. Desserts

9. Thank You

Introduction

Welcome to "Easy Eats for Teens," a cookbook designed espe- cially for young aspiring chefs looking to embark on a culinary journey filled with delicious adventures! Whether you're a novice in the kitchen or already have some cooking experience, this cookbook is here to make the art of cooking accessible, enjoyable, and rewarding for teenagers like you.

In this cookbook, we recognize that the teenage years are a time of discovery, growth, and increasing independence. Learning to cook isn't just about creating tasty meals; it's about gaining essential life skills that will serve you well throughout your life. "Easy Eats for Teens" is your passport to exploring the world of cooking, one step at a time, and discovering the joy of preparing your own meals.

Cooking is not only a valuable life skill but also a fantastic way to express your creativity, experiment with flavors, and share memorable moments with friends and family. By using this cookbook, you'll learn how to whip up a variety of scrumptious dishes that will impress your taste buds and those of your loved ones.

Throughout the pages of "Easy Eats for Teens," you'll find a curated collection of recipes that are specifically chosen for their simplicity and deliciousness. From quick and nutritious breakfasts to satisfying lunches, delectable snacks, and even special occasion treats, there's something here for every taste and occasion.

But this cookbook is about more than just recipes. It's about building confidence in the kitchen, understanding the basics of cooking techniques, and fostering a sense of independence. We'll guide you through essential kitchen skills, from measuring ingredients accurately to practicing kitchen safety and hygiene. By mastering these fundamentals, you'll have the confidence to experiment with your own culinary creations.

So, grab your apron, roll up your sleeves, and let's get started on this exciting culinary adventure together. "Easy Eats for Teens" is here to inspire you, support you, and help you become a confident and skilled young chef. Get ready to savor the satisfaction of preparing and enjoying your very own homemade meals!

Kitchen Essentials

Basic Kitchen Safety and Hygiene Tips

In the world of cooking, safety and hygiene should always be your top priority. The kitchen can be a wonderful place for creativity, but it can also present potential hazards. To ensure your cooking experience is not only enjoyable but also safe, follow these essential kitchen safety and hygiene tips:

1. Wash Your Hands: Before you begin cooking, make it a habit to wash your hands thoroughly with soap and warm water for at least 20 seconds. This helps prevent the spread of germs and keeps your food clean.

2. Clean as You Go: Keep your workspace neat and tidy. Clean up spills immediately, and regularly wipe down countertops, cutting boards, and utensils to prevent cross- contamination.

3. Use the Right Tools: Make sure you're using the appropri- ate utensils and equipment for the task at hand. Using the wrong tools can be dangerous and lead to accidents.

4. Learn Knife Safety: Proper knife skills are crucial. Always cut away from yourself, keep your fingers tucked in, and use a sharp knife to reduce the risk of accidents.

5. Handle Hot Items with Care: When working with hot pots, pans, or baking sheets, use oven mitts or pot holders to protect your hands. Always be mindful of hot surfaces.

6. Avoid Loose Clothing: Loose clothing can easily catch fire or get caught on handles and knobs. Wear fitted clothing or roll up your sleeves when cooking.

7. Keep Flammable Items Away: Keep flammable items like paper towels, dish towels, and curtains away from the stove, oven, and other hot surfaces.

8. Be Cautious with Steam: When opening lids or pots with steam, do so away from your face and body to avoid burns.

9. Watch for Allergens: If you or someone you're cook- ing for has food allergies, be extra vigilant about cross- contamination and read ingredient labels carefully.

10. Safe Food Storage: Refrigerate perishable foods promptly and ensure that your refrigerator is at the appropriate temperature (below 40°F or 4°C). Label leftovers with dates to track freshness.

11. Learn About Fire Safety: Familiarize yourself with how to use a fire extinguisher, and know the location of fire exits in your kitchen and home.

12. Educate Yourself: Take the time to learn about food safety guidelines and safe cooking temperatures to prevent food- borne illnesses.

13. Never Leave Cooking Unattended: Whether you're frying, baking, or simmering, always stay in the kitchen while cooking. Unattended cooking is a leading cause of kitchen fires.

14. Ask for Help When Needed: If you're unsure about a cooking technique or need assistance, don't hesitate to ask an experienced adult or guardian for guidance.

By following these kitchen safety and hygiene tips, you'll not only protect yourself and others but also enjoy a more confident and enjoyable cooking experience. Remember, safety first, and happy cooking!

List of Essential Kitchen Tools and Equipment

Setting up a well-equipped kitchen is the first step to becoming a confident and efficient cook. While there are countless kitchen gadgets and utensils available, you don't need them all. Here's a list of essential kitchen tools and equipment that will cover most of your cooking needs:

1. Chef's Knife: Invest in a good-quality chef's knife for chopping, slicing, and dicing. It's one of the most versatile tools in the kitchen.

2. Paring Knife: A smaller knife for more delicate tasks like peeling and trimming.

3. Cutting Board: Use a durable and easy-to-clean cutting board to protect your countertops and keep your knives sharp.

4. Mixing Bowls: A set of various-sized mixing bowls for mixing, tossing, and storing ingredients.

5. Measuring Cups and Spoons: For precise measurements of dry and liquid ingredients.

6. Saucepan: A medium-sized saucepan with a lid for boiling, simmering, and making sauces.

7. Frying Pan (Skillet): A versatile pan for sautéing, frying, and making omelets.

8. Stockpot: A large, deep pot for boiling pasta, making soups, and cooking larger quantities of food.

9. Baking Sheet: A flat, rimmed sheet for baking cookies, roasting vegetables, and more.

10. Ovenproof Casserole Dish: Ideal for baking casseroles, lasagnas, and other oven dishes.

11. Colander or Strainer: For draining pasta, rinsing vegeta- bles, and straining liquids.

12. Whisk: Use for blending, whipping, and incorporating air into mixtures.

13. Spatula: Essential for flipping pancakes, burgers, and delicate foods.

14. Tongs: A versatile tool for turning meat, tossing salads, and serving.

15. Wooden Spoon: Great for stirring, scraping, and mixing without scratching cookware.

16. Can Opener: For opening canned goods.

17. Peeler: Makes peeling fruits and vegetables quick and easy.

18. Grater: Use for grating cheese, vegetables, and citrus zest.

19. Microwave-Safe Bowl: For heating and reheating food in the microwave.

20. Timer: Handy for keeping track of cooking times, espe- cially when multitasking.

21. Baking Dish: For baking casseroles, brownies, and desserts.

22. Kitchen Thermometer: Ensures meats and baked goods are cooked to the right temperature.

23. Kitchen Towels and Oven Mitts: Protect your hands and handle hot items safely.

24. Canisters or Airtight Containers: For storing dry ingredi- ents like flour, sugar, and pasta.

25. Meat Mallet: Used for pounding meat to an even thickness for cooking.

26. Rolling Pin: Essential for rolling out dough for pies, cookies, and pastries.

27. Silicone Spatula: Perfect for scraping bowls and pans, and ideal for non-stick cookware.

28. Food Processor or Blender: Optional but convenient for chopping, pureeing, and blending.

29. Mixer (Hand or Stand): Useful for mixing and whipping ingredients, especially for baking.

Start with these basic kitchen tools and equipment, and as you gain more experience, you can add specia- lized items to your collection. Remember that the key is to choose high-quality, durable items that will serve you well over time. Happy cooking!

Tips for Organizing and Maintaining a Functional Kitchen Space

A well-organized kitchen not only makes cooking more enjoy- able but also increases efficiency and reduces stress. Here are some tips to help you keep your kitchen space functional and tidy:

1. Declutter Regularly: Go through your kitchen cabinets and drawers periodically to declutter. Donate or discard items you no longer use or need. Keeping a clutter-free kitchen makes it easier to find what you're looking for.

2. Designate Zones: Organize your kitchen into specific zones based on function. For example, have a baking zone with all your baking tools and ingredients, a prep zone with cutting boards and knives, and a cooking zone near the stove.

3. Use Drawer Organizers: Invest in drawer dividers and organizers to keep utensils, measuring spoons, and other small items neat and easily accessible.

4. Maximize Vertical Space: Install shelves or hooks on your kitchen walls to store pots, pans, and utensils. This frees up valuable cabinet space and adds a decorative element to your kitchen.

5. Trash Bowl: Keep a designated "trash bowl" on your countertop while cooking. This saves you trips to the trash can and helps maintain a clean workspace. Empty it into the trash when you're finished.

6. Label Containers: Use clear, airtight containers to store pantry items like flour, sugar, and pasta. Label them for easy identification and to keep ingredients fresh.

7. Organize Spices: Arrange your spices in alphabetical order or by cuisine type. Consider a spice rack or drawer insert to maximize space and visibility.

8. Fridge and Freezer Organization: Regularly clean out your refrigerator and freezer, disposing of expired items. Use clear bins and labels to separate and identify foods.

9. Keep Like Items Together: Store similar items together, such as pots with lids, cutting boards with knives, and baking sheets with cooling racks.

10. Group by Frequency of Use: Place frequently used items at eye level and less-used items on higher or lower shelves. This ensures easy access to the items you use most.

11. Rotate Stock: When restocking groceries, place newer items behind older ones to use older items first and reduce food waste.

12. Regular Cleaning: Develop a cleaning routine to wipe down countertops, appliances, and the sink daily. Don't forget to clean the stovetop and microwave after use.

13. Use Drawer Liners: Protect your drawers from scratches and make them easier to clean by adding non-slip drawer liners.

14. Vertical Plate Rack: Use a vertical plate rack or holder to stack plates, cutting down on clutter in your cabinets.

15. Appliance Storage: Store small appliances, like blenders or stand mixers, in dedicated cabinets or on pull-out shelves to free up counter space.

16. Maintain a Dish Rack: Invest in a dish rack or drying mat to keep washed dishes and utensils organized while they dry.

17. Purge Expired Items: Regularly check for expired or stale foods in your pantry and refrigerator. Dispose of them to make room for fresh items.

By implementing these organization tips and keeping a trash bowl handy, you'll create an efficient and enjoyable kitchen environment that makes cooking a breeze. A well-organized kitchen not only saves you time but also makes it more inviting to explore new recipes and culinary adventures.

Common Cooking Terms and Techniques

Cooking involves a language all its own, filled with various terms and techniques that can be a bit intimidating to beginners. To help you feel more confident in the kitchen, let's explore some common cooking terms and techniques that you're likely to encounter:

1. Sauté: To cook food quickly in a small amount of oil or butter over high heat, often in a skillet or sauté pan. It's used for quickly cooking vegetables, meats, or other ingredients while maintaining their texture and flavor.

2. Simmer: To cook food gently in liquid at a temperature just below boiling. This technique is commonly used for soups, stews, and sauces.

3. Boil: To cook food in liquid at a temperature where the liquid vigorously bubbles and rolls. Boiling is often used for pasta, vegetables, and grains.

4. Roast: To cook food, typically meat, poultry, or vegetables, in an oven at a high temperature, resulting in a browned, flavorful exterior and moist interior.

5. Grill: To cook food over an open flame or heat source, usually on a grill or barbecue. Grilling imparts a smoky flavor and distinctive grill marks.

6. Bake: To cook food, especially baked goods like bread, cakes, and cookies, in an oven using dry heat. Baking relies on consistent temperature for even cooking.

7. Broil: To cook food by exposing it to direct heat from above. Broiling is often used to brown the top of dishes like casseroles or to quickly cook items like steaks.

8. Blanch: To briefly immerse food in boiling water, followed by rapid cooling in ice water. Blanching is used to soften vegetables, remove skins, or set colors.

9. Poach: To gently cook food, usually eggs or delicate proteins like fish, in simmering liquid until just cooked through.

10. Sear: To cook food over high heat in a hot pan to create a flavorful, caramelized crust. This is often done with meat or fish.

11. Grate: To shred food into small, fine pieces using a grater. This is commonly done with cheese, vegetables, and citrus zest.

12. Whisk: To beat ingredients together vigorously using a whisk to incorporate air and create a smooth mixture. This is used for making sauces, dressings, and batters.

13. Fold: To gently combine two ingredients, usually a lighter mixture into a denser one, by using a gentle lifting and turning motion. This technique is commonly used in baking and making mousse or soufflés.

14. Dice: To cut food into small, uniform pieces. Common dice sizes include small dice, medium dice, and large dice.

15. Julienne: To cut food into thin, matchstick-sized strips. This technique is often used for vegetables in salads and stir- fries.

16. Mince: To chop food into very fine pieces, often used for garlic, onions, and herbs.

17. Reduce: To simmer a liquid, such as a sauce or stock, to evaporate some of the water content, resulting in a thicker and more concentrated flavor.

18. Deglaze: To add liquid (often wine or broth) to a hot pan to loosen and incorporate the flavorful browned bits left after cooking meat. This is used to make sauces.

19. Marinate: To soak food in a flavorful liquid mixture, typically containing herbs, spices, and acids like vinegar or citrus juice, to infuse it with flavor and tenderize it.

20. Rest: To allow cooked meat to sit for a few minutes after removing it from heat, which helps redistribute juices for a juicier result when sliced.

Learning these common cooking terms and techniques is like learning a new language that will open up a world of culinary possibilities. As you gain experience, you'll become more comfortable with these concepts and be able to experiment with your own creative recipes. Happy cooking!

Step-by-Step Guide on How to Measure Ingredients

Accurate measurement of ingredients is the foundation of successful cooking and baking. Follow this step--by-step guide to ensure your ingredients are measured correctly and that your recipes turn out as intended:

1. Gather Your Tools:

- Before you begin, make sure you have the necessary measur- ing tools on hand. These typically include measuring cups, measuring spoons, a kitchen scale, and a liquid measuring cup.

2. Use the Correct Measuring Tools:

- Choose the appropriate measuring tool for the ingredient you're working with. For dry ingredients like flour and sugar, use dry measuring cups. For liquids, use liquid measuring cups. Measuring spoons are for small quantities of dry or liquid ingredients.

3. Set Up Your Work Area:

- Clear your workspace and ensure it's clean and dry. Place your measuring tools, ingredients, and the recipe you're following nearby for easy reference.

4. Measure Dry Ingredients:

- For dry ingredients like flour, sugar, or cocoa powder: a. Fluff up the ingredient by stirring it with a spoon or a scoop. b. Gently spoon the ingredient into the measuring cup, overfilling it slightly. c. Use a straight-edged utensil, like the back of a knife, to level off the excess by sweeping it across the top of the measuring cup. Do not tap the cup; this can lead to inaccurate measurements.

5. Measure Liquid Ingredients:

- For liquids like water, milk, or oil: a. Place the liquid measuring cup on a level surface. b. Pour the liquid into the measuring cup, filling it to the desired level. Check the measurement at eye level for accuracy. Liquid measure- ments are read at the meniscus, which is the curved surface of the liquid.

6. Measure Small Quantities:

- For small quantities, use measuring spoons. Dip the spoon into the ingredient and level it off with a straight-edged utensil, just like with dry measuring cups.

7. Use a Kitchen Scale (Optional):

- A kitchen scale provides precise measurements, especially for ingredients like flour, where accuracy is crucial. Place your container on the scale, tare it to zero, and then add the desired amount of the ingredient.

8. Measure Sticky Ingredients:

- For sticky ingredients like honey or peanut butter: a. Lightly grease the measuring cup or spoon with cooking spray or oil. b. Pour or scoop the sticky ingredient into the greased measuring tool, ensuring it levels off properly.

9. Read the Recipe Carefully:

· Always refer to your recipe for specific measurement in- structions. Some recipes may call for ingredients measured by weight (grams or ounces) rather than volume (cups).

10. Double-Check Your Measurements:

· Before adding the ingredients to your mixing bowl or pot, double-check your measurements to ensure accuracy. This is especially important in baking, where precision matters.

By following this step-by-step guide, you'll be well on your way to mastering the art of measuring ingredients accurately. Consistent and precise measurements will help you achieve consistent and delicious results in your cooking and baking adventures.

Basic Cooking Methods

Cooking is an art, and mastering different cooking methods is like having a palette of techniques at your disposal to create a wide range of flavors, textures, and dishes. Here are some basic cooking methods to help you understand the fundamentals of cooking:

1. Sautéing:

   · Description: Sautéing involves cooking small pieces of food quickly in a small amount of hot oil or butter in a pan or skillet. It's a versatile method used for vegetables, meat, and seafood.

   · Tips: Use high heat and keep the ingredients moving by tossing or stirring to prevent burning.

2. Boiling:

   · Description: Boiling is the process of cooking food by im- mersing it in boiling water or another liquid. It's commonly used for pasta, rice, vegetables, and eggs.

   · Tips: Use a large pot, add salt to the water for flavor, and cook until the food is tender but not overcooked.

3. Roasting:

   · Description: Roasting involves cooking food, often meat or vegetables, in an oven at high tempera- tures. It results in a browned, flavorful exterior and a moist interior.

   · Tips: Preheat the oven, use a roasting pan or baking sheet, and periodically baste the food with its juices or marinade.

4. Grilling:

   · Description: Grilling is cooking food directly over an open flame or heat source, such as a grill or barbecue. It imparts a smoky flavor and is great for meats, seafood, and vegetables.

   · Tips: Preheat the grill, clean and oil the grates, and turn the food at appropriate intervals for even cooking.

5. Baking:

   · Description: Baking is cooking food, especially baked goods like bread, cakes, and cookies, in an oven using dry heat. It relies on consistent temperature for even cooking.

   · Tips: Follow recipes carefully, preheat the oven, and use the middle rack for even heat distribution.

6. Frying:

   · Description: Frying involves cooking food in hot oil or fat. There are two main types: deep frying, where food is submerged in oil, and shallow frying, where food is partially submerged.

   · Tips: Use a deep fryer or a heavy skillet with enough oil to fully or partially cover the food. Maintain the correct oil temperature to achieve a crispy texture.

7. Steaming:

   · Description: Steaming involves cooking food by exposing it to steam. It's a gentle method that preserves the food's nutrients and flavors, often used for vegetables, fish, and dumplings.

- Tips: Use a steamer basket or a microwave-safe container with a lid. Make sure there's enough water to generate steam without touching the food.

8. Simmering:

- Description: Simmering is cooking food gently in liquid at a temperature just below boiling. It's commonly used for soups, stews, and braises.

- Tips: Maintain a low, steady heat to prevent rapid boiling. Cover the pot to retain moisture and flavors.

9. Braising:

- Description: Braising is a two-step cooking method that involves searing food at high heat and then simmering it in a flavorful liquid. It's great for tougher cuts of meat and vegetables.

- Tips: Sear the food to develop a rich flavor, then add liquid and simmer it slowly until tender.

10. Poaching:

- Description: Poaching is gently cooking food, usually eggs or delicate proteins like fish, in simmering liquid until just cooked through. It's used to maintain the food's shape and tenderness.

- Tips: Use a flavored poaching liquid for added taste, and keep the temperature just below simmering to prevent overcooking.

Each of these basic cooking methods offers a unique set of advantages and can be adapted to various ingredients and cuisines. As you gain experience, you'll develop a deeper understanding of when and how to use these techniques to create delicious dishes.

Breakfast Basics

Fried Egg

Ingredients:

- 1 large egg
- Butter or cooking oil (about 1 tablespoon)
- Salt and pepper (optional)

Instructions:

1. Prepare Your Utensils:
- Gather all the necessary utensils: a non-stick skillet or frying pan, a spatula, and a plate.

2. Heat the Pan:
- Place the skillet or frying pan on the stovetop over low to medium-low heat. Allow it to heat up for a minute or two. Adding a small amount of butter or oil will help prevent sticking and add flavor.

3. Crack the Egg:
- While the pan is heating, crack the egg into a small bowl or cup. Be careful not to get any shell fragments into the bowl.

4. Add Butter or Oil:
- Once the pan is hot, add about 1 tablespoon of butter or cooking oil and let it melt and coat the bottom of the pan evenly.

5. Fry the Egg:
- Gently slide the cracked egg into the hot pan.

6. Season (Optional):
- If desired, sprinkle a pinch of salt and pepper over the egg. You can also add seasonings like herbs or grated cheese for extra flavor.

7. Cook to Your Preference:
- For sunny-side-up eggs, cover the pan with a lid and cook until the whites are set but the yolk is still runny, about 2-3 minutes. You can spoon some of the hot butter or oil over the egg to help cook the top.

8. Flip (Optional):
- If you prefer an over-easy or over-medium egg, carefully flip it using a spatula after about 2-3 minutes to cook the other side.

9. Plate and Serve:
- Slide the fried egg onto a plate.

10. Enjoy:

· Serve your fried egg hot, as is or with your choice of sides like toast, bacon, or sautéed vegetables.

Frying an egg is a simple and versatile cooking skill that's perfect for new cooks. Adjust the cooking time to achieve your preferred level of doneness for the yolk. With practice, you can master the art of frying eggs to perfection.

Perfect Hard-Boiled Eggs

Hard-boiled eggs are versatile and can be used in salads, sand- wiches, or as a healthy snack. Here's a step-by-step guide to making perfect hard-boiled eggs:

Ingredients:

- Eggs (as many as you need)
- Water
- Ice

Equipment:

- Saucepan with a lid
- Slotted spoon

Instructions:

1. Choose the Right Eggs:
- Start with fresh eggs. The fresher the eggs, the easier they will be to peel.
2. Boil Water:
- Place your eggs in a single layer in a saucepan. Add enough water to the saucepan to cover the eggs by about an inch.
3. Boil the Water:
- Place the saucepan over high heat and bring the water to a rolling boil.
4. Add Salt (Optional):
- You can add a pinch of salt to the boiling water, which may help make the eggs easier to peel. This step is optional.
5. Lower the Heat:
- As soon as the water reaches a rolling boil, reduce the heat to low and let it simmer gently for 9-12 minutes, depending on your desired level of doneness:
- 9 minutes for slightly soft yolks (ideal for ramen or salads)
- 10-12 minutes for fully set yolks (perfect for salads, sand- wiches, or deviled eggs)
6. Prepare an Ice Bath:
- While the eggs are simmering, fill a large bowl with ice and cold water.
7. Remove the Eggs:
- When the eggs are done, use a slotted spoon to carefully transfer them from the saucepan to the ice bath immediately. This helps stop the cooking process and makes the eggs easier to peel.

8. Cool the Eggs:

- Let the eggs sit in the ice bath for at least 5-10 minutes to cool completely. This ensures that the yolks set properly and prevents the greenish-gray ring from forming around the yolk.

9. Peel the Eggs:

- Once the eggs are cool, gently tap them on a hard surface to crack the shell. Roll them between your hands to loosen the shell. Start peeling from the wider end (where the air pocket is), as it's usually easier to remove the shell from there.

10. Store or Enjoy:

- You can store your hard-boiled eggs in the refrigerator for up to one week. Enjoy them sliced, diced, or as a whole egg.

11. Tips:

- Using a slotted spoon to transfer the eggs from the boiling water to the ice bath helps prevent cracked shells and makes for easier peeling.

- Older eggs are easier to peel because the pH level in the egg whites rises as they age.

- You can test the level of doneness by spinning a cooled egg on a countertop. If it spins easily, it's hard-boiled; if it wobbles, it's softer.

Perfectly boiled eggs are a kitchen staple and can be used in a variety of dishes. Mastering this basic cooking technique is a valuable skill for any home chef.

Poached Eggs

Poaching an egg is a simple technique that results in a perfectly cooked, silky, and runny yolk encased in a delicate white. Here's a step-by-step guide on how to poach an egg:

Ingredients:

- Fresh eggs (as many as you need)
- Water
- Vinegar (optional)
- Salt (optional)

Equipment:

- A small bowl or ramekin
- A slotted spoon
- A saucepan or deep skillet
- A timer or watch

Instructions:

1. Prepare the Water:

- Fill a saucepan or deep skillet with water, about 2-3 inches deep. You don't need a lot of water; just enough to cover the eggs.

2. Heat the Water:

- Place the saucepan over medium heat and bring the water to a gentle simmer. You should see small bubbles forming at the bottom of the pan, but the water should not be boiling vigorously.

3. Crack the Egg:

- Crack a fresh egg into a small bowl or ramekin. Be careful not to break the yolk.

4. Add Vinegar (Optional):

- If you like, you can add a teaspoon of vinegar (white or apple cider vinegar) to the simmering water. This helps coagulate the egg whites faster, resulting in a neater poached egg. However, this step is optional.

5. Create a Whirlpool (Optional):

- To help the egg whites wrap around the yolk, you can gently stir the simmering water in a circular motion using a spoon, creating a whirlpool effect.

6. Slide the Egg In:

- Hold the small bowl or ramekin with the cracked egg close to the surface of the simmering water.
- Carefully slide the egg into the center of the swirling water. The whirlpool effect will help the egg whites wrap around the yolk.

7. Poach the Egg:

- Let the egg cook undisturbed for about 3-4 minutes for a runny yolk. Adjust the cooking time slightly for your desired yolk consistency:
- 3 minutes for a runny yolk
- 4 minutes for a slightly firmer yolk
- 5 minutes for a yolk that's still soft but not runny
- 6 minutes for a medium-firm yolk

8. Remove the Poached Egg:

- Use a slotted spoon to gently lift the poached egg out of the water. Allow any excess water to drain off.

9. Season and Serve:

- Season the poached egg with a pinch of salt and black pepper, if desired.
- Serve your perfectly poached egg on a bed of spinach, on a slice of toast, or as a topping for dishes like eggs Benedict or salads.

10. Enjoy:

- Break into the poached egg with a fork, and enjoy the creamy yolk goodness!

11. Tips:

- Use the freshest eggs you can find for the best results. Fresher eggs have firmer whites that hold their shape better during poaching.
- Experiment with different cooking times to achieve your preferred yolk consistency.
- You can poach multiple eggs at once by repeating the process for each egg, but make sure not to overcrowd the pan.

Poaching eggs may seem intimidating at first, but with practice, you'll master this technique and be able to enjoy delicious poached eggs anytime you like.

Classic Scrambled Eggs

Prep Time: 2 minutes | Cook Time: 3-5 minutes | Total Time: 5-7 minutes

Serving Size: 2 servings

Ingredients:

- 4 large eggs
- Salt, to taste
- Black pepper, to taste
- 2 tablespoons butter

Instructions:

1. Crack and Whisk the Eggs:

- Crack the eggs into a bowl, and season with a pinch of salt and a dash of black pepper. You can add a tablespoon of milk or cream for creamier eggs, but it's optional.
- Use a fork or whisk to beat the eggs until the yolks and whites are fully combined, and the mixture is slightly frothy. Be sure not to overbeat; a gentle mix is all you need.

2. Preheat the Skillet:

- Place a non-stick skillet over medium-low heat. Allow it to heat up for a minute or two.

3. Add Butter:

- Add the butter to the skillet and let it melt. Swirl it around to coat the bottom evenly. The butter will sizzle slightly but should not brown.

4. Cook the Eggs:

- Pour the beaten eggs into the skillet with the melted butter.
- Let the eggs cook undisturbed for a few seconds until you see the edges starting to set.
- Gently stir the eggs with a spatula, pushing them from the edges towards the center. Continue stirring and folding the eggs occasionally.
- Cook the eggs until they are just set but still slightly creamy. This should take about 3-5 minutes in total. Remember that the eggs will continue to cook for a moment even after you've turned off the heat, so it's better to slightly undercook them in the pan.

5. Serve Immediately:

- As soon as the eggs reach your desired level of doneness (they should be soft and slightly runny), remove them from the skillet.
- Transfer the scrambled eggs to a plate immediately to stop the cooking process. They should be creamy, fluffy, and moist.

6. Season and Enjoy:

- Taste the scrambled eggs and adjust the seasoning with a pinch more salt and black pepper if needed.
- Serve your classic scrambled eggs hot, garnished with fresh herbs like chives, parsley, or a sprinkle of grated cheese if you prefer.

Enjoy your classic scrambled eggs for a delicious and quick breakfast or brunch!

Omelette

Prep Time: 5 minutes Cook Time: 5 minutes Total Time: 10 minutes

Serving Size: 1 omelette

Ingredients:

- 2-3 large eggs
- Salt and black pepper, to taste
- 1-2 tablespoons butter or cooking oil
- 1/4 cup grated cheese (e.g., cheddar, Swiss, or your favorite)
- 1/4 cup diced vegetables (e.g., bell peppers, onions, toma- toes, mushrooms, or spinach)
- 1/4 cup diced ham or cooked bacon bits (optional)
- Fresh herbs (e.g., parsley or chives, for garnish)

Instructions:

1. Prepare Your Fillings:

- Dice your choice of vegetables and any other fillings you'd like to use (cheese, ham, bacon, etc.).

2. Beat the Eggs:

- Crack the eggs into a bowl. Add a pinch of salt and a dash of black pepper to season. Use a fork or whisk to beat the eggs until the yolks and whites are well combined and slightly frothy.

3. Heat the Skillet:

- Place a non-stick skillet over medium-high heat. Add the butter or cooking oil and let it melt, ensuring the skillet is evenly coated.

4. Pour the Eggs:

- Once the butter is hot and foamy (but not browned), pour the beaten eggs into the skillet.

5. Swirl and Cook:

- Use a spatula to gently push the cooked edges of the eggs towards the center while tilting the skillet to let the un- cooked eggs flow to the edges. Continue this process until the omelette is mostly set but still slightly runny on top.

6. Add Fillings:

- Sprinkle your chosen fillings (cheese, diced vegetables, ham, etc.) evenly over one half of the omelette.

7. Fold and Serve:

- When the eggs are mostly set but still slightly runny on top, carefully fold the other half of the omelette over the fillings. Use your spatula to gently fold it in half.

8. Finish Cooking:

- Let the omelette cook for another minute or so, until the cheese is melted, and the omelette is cooked to your desired level of doneness. It should be slightly golden on the outside but still moist on the inside.

9. Slide onto a Plate:

- Carefully slide the omelette onto a plate, folding it in half if necessary.

10. Garnish and Serve:

- Garnish your omelette with fresh herbs, such as chopped parsley or chives, for added flavor and presentation.

11. Enjoy:

- Serve your delicious omelette hot and enjoy your customized breakfast!

Variations:

- The filling options for omelettes are limitless. Feel free to experiment with different combinations of vegetables, cheeses, meats, and herbs to create your favorite omelette.

- For a healthier option, you can use egg whites or a mix of whole eggs and egg whites.

- If you prefer a creamier texture, you can add a splash of milk or cream to the beaten eggs before cooking.

Oven Cooked Bacon

Ingredients:

- Slices of bacon

Instructions:

1. Preheat the Oven (Optional):

- Preheat your oven to 375°F (190°C). This method is great for cooking larger quantities of bacon evenly.

2. Prepare a Baking Sheet (Optional):

- If you're using the oven method, line a baking sheet with aluminum foil for easy cleanup. You can also place a wire rack on the baking sheet to elevate the bacon.

3. Arrange the Bacon:

- Lay the bacon slices on the baking sheet or in a cold skillet, making sure they don't overlap.

4. Cook in the Oven (Optional):

- If using the oven, place the bacon in the preheated oven and cook for about 15-20 minutes, or until it reaches your desired level of crispiness. Keep an eye on it to prevent overcooking, as cooking times may vary depending on your oven and the thickness of the bacon.

5. Cook on the Stovetop (Alternative):

- If you prefer stovetop cooking, start with a cold skillet. Place the bacon slices in the skillet in a single layer. Turn the heat to medium-low.

6. Flip the Bacon (Stovetop Method):

- As the bacon starts to sizzle and curl at the edges, use tongs or a fork to flip the slices occasionally for even cooking. Continue cooking until it reaches your desired level of crispiness, typically 5-10 minutes.

7. Transfer and Drain:

- Once the bacon is cooked to your liking, remove it from the oven or skillet. Place it on a plate lined with paper towels to absorb excess grease.

8. Serve:

- Serve the crispy bacon slices as a side dish, in sandwiches, salads, or any recipe that calls for bacon.

9. Store Leftovers:

- If you have leftover cooked bacon, let it cool completely. Then, store it in an airtight container in the refrigerator for up to a few days. You can reheat it in the microwave or oven when needed.

Cooking bacon is a straightforward process, and you can adjust the cooking time to achieve the level of crispiness you prefer. Whether you cook it in the oven or on the stovetop, the result is delicious crispy bacon that can be enjoyed in a variety of dishes or on its own.

Ingredients:

- Breakfast sausages (pork, turkey, or your preferred type)
- Cooking oil (such as vegetable or canola oil, if needed)

Instructions:

10. Select Your Sausages:

- Choose your preferred breakfast sausages. You can use pork, turkey, chicken, or any other variety you like.

11. Check for Casing:

- Some sausages come in casings. If your sausages have casings, you can choose to remove them or leave them on. To remove the casing, simply make a shallow cut down the length of the sausage and peel the casing away. If you prefer to leave it on, prick the sausages with a fork to prevent them from bursting during cooking.

12. Preheat the Pan:

- Place a non-stick skillet or frying pan on the stove and heat it over medium heat. If you're using sausages with a higher fat content, you may not need to add any cooking oil. However, if you're using leaner sausages, you can add a small amount of oil to the pan to prevent sticking.

13. Add Sausages to the Pan:

- Carefully place the sausages in the hot skillet. Leave enough space between them to allow for even cooking. Avoid overcrowding the pan.

14. Cook the Sausages:

- Let the sausages cook undisturbed for about 4-5 minutes on one side. You'll notice them start to brown and sizzle.

15. Flip the Sausages:

- Use tongs to gently flip the sausages to the other side. Continue cooking for another 4-5 minutes or until they are browned and cooked through.

16. Check for Doneness:

- To ensure the sausages are fully cooked, use a meat ther- mometer to check their internal temperature. Breakfast sausages should reach an internal temperature of 160°F (71°C).

17. Remove from Heat:

- Once the sausages are cooked to the desired temperature and have a golden-brown exterior, remove them from the heat.

18. Rest and Serve:

- Allow the sausages to rest for a few minutes before serving. This helps retain their juices and flavor.

19. Serve:

- Plate your cooked breakfast sausages and enjoy them along- side scrambled eggs, pancakes, or any other breakfast items you like.

Cooking breakfast sausages is a straightforward process, mak- ing it an excellent option for a first-time cook. Just ensure they are cooked to the recommended internal temperature for safety and enjoy your delicious breakfast!

Eggs in the Basket

Prep Time: 5 minutes | Cook Time: 10 minutes | Total Time: 15 minutes

Serving Size: 2 servings

Ingredients:

- 4 slices of bread (white, whole wheat, or your choice)
- 4 large eggs
- 2 tablespoons butter
- Salt and black pepper, to taste
- Fresh herbs (optional, for garnish)

Instructions:

1. Prepare the Bread:

- Butter one side of the bread. Use a round cookie cutter or a drinking glass with a diameter of about 2.5 inches to cut a hole in the center of each slice of bread. Keep the removed bread circles for toasting later.

2. Cook:

- Melt butter in skillet over medium heat until it covers the bottom.
- Once the butter is hot, carefully place each slice of bread in the skillet unbuttered side down.
- Crack an egg into the hole in the center of each slice of bread. Season with a pinch of salt and a dash of black pepper.
- Cook the eggs for about 3-4 minutes on one side until the whites appear to be set on the other side and the bread is brown. Flip the bread and egg to cook the other side for an additional minute or so.

3. Serve:

- Carefully remove the Eggs in the Basket from the skillet using a spatula.
- Garnish with fresh herbs if desired.

4. Enjoy:

- Serve your Eggs in the Basket hot and enjoy the delightful combination of crispy bread and perfectly cooked eggs!

Variations:

- For a spicy kick, sprinkle some hot sauce or red pepper flakes on top of the eggs.

Eggs in the Basket, also known as "Toad in the Hole," is a fun and delicious breakfast dish that's easy to make and perfect for a cozy morning meal.

Overnight Oats

Prep Time: 5 minutes | Chill Time: At least 4 hours or overnight | Total Time: 4 hours and 5 minutes (or overnight)

Serving Size: 1 serving

Ingredients:

- 1/2 cup rolled oats (old-fashioned oats)
- 1/2 cup milk (dairy or non-dairy, like almond milk, soy milk, or oat milk)
- 1/4 cup Greek yogurt (plain or flavored)
- 1-2 tablespoons honey or maple syrup (adjust to your sweetness preference)
- 1/2 teaspoon vanilla extract (optional)
- Pinch of salt
- Your favorite toppings (e.g., fresh fruit, berries, nuts, seeds, dried fruit, chocolate chips, or nut butter)

Instructions:

1. Assemble the Base:
- In a mason jar or a container with a lid, combine the rolled oats, milk, Greek yogurt, honey or maple syrup, vanilla extract (if using), and a pinch of salt.

2. Mix Well:
- Stir all the ingredients together until well combined. Ensure that the oats are fully soaked in the liquid.

3. Add Toppings:
- Customize your overnight oats by adding your favorite toppings. Here are some ideas:
- Fresh fruit: Sliced bananas, berries, chopped apples, or diced mangoes.
- Nuts and seeds: Almonds, walnuts, chia seeds, flaxseeds, or pumpkin seeds.
- Dried fruit: Raisins, cranberries, or apricots.
- Sweeteners: A drizzle of additional honey or maple syrup.
- Flavorings: Cinnamon, nutmeg, or cocoa powder for extra flavor.

4. Seal and Refrigerate:
- Seal the mason jar or container with a lid.
- Place the overnight oats in the refrigerator and let them chill for at least 4 hours, but ideally overnight. This allows the oats to absorb the liquid and soften.

5. Serve:

· When you're ready to enjoy your overnight oats, remove them from the fridge.

· Give the oats a good stir to combine all the ingredients and ensure the mixture is creamy and well--mixed.

· If desired, add a bit more milk to adjust the consistency to your liking.

· Top your overnight oats with additional fresh fruit, nuts, or a drizzle of honey for extra flavor and texture.

6. Enjoy:

· Dive into your delicious, convenient, and nutritious overnight oats for a quick and satisfying breakfast.

Note: Overnight oats can be made in advance and stored in the refrigerator for up to 2-3 days. They are a great option for busy mornings when you need a healthy and filling breakfast on the go.

Avocado Toast

Prep Time: 5 minutes | Total Time: 5 minutes

Serving Size: 1 serving

Ingredients:

- 1 ripe avocado
- 2 slices of whole-grain bread
- Salt, to taste
- Black pepper, to taste
- Red pepper flakes (optional, for a spicy kick)
- Lemon juice (optional, for extra flavor)

Instructions:

1. Prepare the Avocado:
- Cut the ripe avocado in half, remove the pit, and scoop the flesh into a bowl.
2. Mash the Avocado:
- Use a fork to mash the avocado until it reaches your desired level of creaminess. Some people prefer it slightly chunky, while others like it completely smooth.
3. Toast the Bread:
- Toast two slices of whole-grain bread until they are golden brown and crispy.
4. Spread the Mashed Avocado:
- Once the toast is ready, spread the mashed avocado evenly onto each slice.
5. Season to Taste:
- Sprinkle a pinch of salt and black pepper over the avocado toast. Adjust the amount to your taste preferences.
6. Add Red Pepper Flakes (Optional):
- If you like a little heat, sprinkle a pinch of red pepper flakes over the avocado toast for some spiciness. Adjust the amount to your spice level preference.
7. Optional: Drizzle with Lemon Juice:
- For an extra burst of flavor and a touch of acidity, you can drizzle a bit of lemon juice over the avocado toast. It enhances the avocado's taste and adds freshness.

8. Serve and Enjoy:

- Your avocado toast is ready to enjoy! Serve it as a quick and satisfying breakfast, snack, or light meal.

Variations:

- Get creative with your avocado toast by adding other top- pings like sliced tomatoes, poached or fried eggs, feta cheese, smoked salmon, or microgreens. You can customize it to your liking and create your favorite flavor combinations.

- Experiment with different types of bread, from sourdough to whole wheat, to find your preferred base for avocado toast.

- f you like additional texture and crunch, sprinkle some toasted seeds (such as sesame seeds or pumpkin seeds) or chopped nuts (like almonds or walnuts) on top of the avocado.

Peanut Butter Banana Toast

Prep Time: 5 minutes | Total Time: 5 minutes

Serving Size: 1 serving

Ingredients:

- 1 slice of whole-grain bread
- 2 tablespoons peanut butter (smooth or crunchy, as per your preference)
- 1 ripe banana, thinly sliced
- Honey or maple syrup for drizzling (optional)
- Cinnamon (optional)

Instructions:

1. Toast the Bread:
- Start by toasting a slice of whole-grain bread to your desired level of crispiness. You can use a toaster or a toaster oven.

2. Spread Peanut Butter:
- While the toast is still warm, spread a generous layer of peanut butter on top. You can use smooth or crunchy peanut butter, depending on your preference.

3. Arrange Banana Slices:
- Place the thinly sliced banana on top of the peanut butter. You can arrange them neatly or simply scatter them across the toast.

4. Optional Additions:
- If you like, drizzle a little honey or maple syrup over the banana slices for added sweetness.
- A sprinkle of ground cinnamon on top can enhance the flavors and add a warm, aromatic touch.

5. Serve and Enjoy:
- Serve your Peanut Butter Banana Toast immediately while it's warm and the peanut butter is slightly melted.
- Enjoy your delicious and satisfying snack or breakfast!

This quick and easy recipe is a classic combination of flavors that provides a perfect balance of creaminess, nuttiness, and natural sweetness. It's not only tasty but also nutritious!

Yogurt Parfait

Prep Time: 5 minutes | Total Time: 5 minutes

Serving Size: 1 serving

Ingredients:

- 1 cup Greek yogurt (plain or flavored)
- 1/2 cup granola (your choice of flavor)
- 1/2 cup fresh berries (e.g., strawberries, blueberries, rasp- berries, or a mix)
- 1 tablespoon honey or maple syrup (optional, for drizzling)
- 1/4 teaspoon vanilla extract (optional)
- A pinch of cinnamon (optional)

Instructions:

1. Choose a Glass or Bowl:
- Select a clear glass or bowl to assemble your yogurt parfait. A clear container will allow you to see the beautiful layers.

2. Layer 1: Greek Yogurt:
- Start by adding a layer of Greek yogurt to the bottom of your glass or bowl. You can use plain Greek yogurt for a classic option or choose a flavored variety for extra sweetness.

3. Layer 2: Granola:
- Next, add a layer of granola on top of the yogurt. You can use your favorite type of granola, whether it's honey almond, vanilla, or any other flavor you prefer.

4. Layer 3: Fresh Berries:
- Place a layer of fresh berries on top of the granola. You can use strawberries, blueberries, raspberries, or a mix of your favorite berries. They add natural sweetness and a burst of color.

5. Optional Additions:
- If you like, drizzle a tablespoon of honey or maple syrup over the berries for extra sweetness.
- For a touch of flavor, add a splash of vanilla extract over the berries or sprinkle a pinch of cinnamon.

6. Repeat Layers:
- Repeat the layers until you've filled your glass or bowl, finishing with a layer of berries on top.

7. Serve and Enjoy:
- Your yogurt parfait is ready to be enjoyed. Use a long spoon to scoop through all the layers and savor the combination of creamy yogurt, crunchy granola, and sweet, juicy berries.

8. Variations:

- Get creative with your yogurt parfait by adding sliced ba- nanas, chopped nuts, or a drizzle of nut butter for extra flavor and texture.

9. Make-Ahead:

- You can prepare yogurt parfaits in advance for a quick and healthy breakfast or snack. Simply cover your glass or bowl with plastic wrap or a lid and refrigerate until you're ready to enjoy.

This yogurt parfait is a versatile and customizable dish that makes a delicious and nutritious breakfast or snack option. Feel free to tailor it to your taste with different yogurt flavors, granola varieties, and fruits.

Fruit Smoothie

Prep Time: 5 minutes | Total Time: 5 minutes

Serving Size: 1 large serving

Ingredients:

- 1 cup frozen mixed fruit (such as berries, mango, or pineap- ple)
- 1/2 cup Greek yogurt (plain or flavored)
- 1/2 cup juice (orange juice, apple juice, or your choice)
- 1 tablespoon honey (optional, for added sweetness)
- 1/4 teaspoon vanilla extract (optional)
- Ice cubes (optional, for a thicker smoothie)
- Fresh fruit or mint leaves for garnish (optional)

Instructions:

1. Gather Your Ingredients:
- Ensure you have all the ingredients ready for easy blending.
2. Add Frozen Fruit:
- Place the frozen mixed fruit into a blender. You can use a store-bought frozen fruit blend or prepare your own by freezing your favorite fruits in advance.
3. Add Greek Yogurt:
- Spoon the Greek yogurt on top of the frozen fruit in the blender.
4. Pour in Juice:
- Pour the juice of your choice over the fruit and yogurt in the blender. This adds a touch of liquid to help with blending.
5. Sweeten and Flavor (Optional):
- If desired, add a tablespoon of honey for added sweetness and a quarter teaspoon of vanilla extract for extra flavor.
6. Add Ice Cubes (Optional):
- If you prefer a thicker smoothie or want to make it extra cold, you can add a few ice cubes to the blender.
7. Blend Until Smooth:
- Secure the blender lid and blend all the ingredients until you have a smooth and creamy mixture. You may need to stop and scrape down the sides or add a bit more juice if it's too thick.

8. Taste and Adjust:

- Taste your smoothie and adjust the sweetness or thickness to your liking. You can add more honey, juice, or ice cubes as needed.

9. Serve:

- Pour your fruit smoothie into a glass.

10. Garnish (Optional):

- If desired, garnish your smoothie with a slice of fresh fruit or a sprig of mint for an extra pop of color and flavor.

11. Enjoy:

- Sip and enjoy your delicious and refreshing fruit smoothie. It's perfect for breakfast, as a snack, or even as a post- workout refreshment.

Variations:

- Get creative with your fruit smoothie by adding other ingre- dients like spinach or kale for a green smoothie, a scoop of protein powder for extra protein, or a spoonful of nut butter for added creami- ness and flavor.

- You can also customize the fruit combination based on your preferences. Experiment with different fruits to create your favorite flavor combinations.

Classic Pancakes

Prep Time: 10 minutes | Cook Time: 15 minutes | Total Time: 25 minutes

Serving Size: Makes approximately 8 pancakes

Ingredients:

- 1 cup all-purpose flour
- 2 tablespoons sugar
- 1 teaspoon baking powder
- 1/2 teaspoon baking soda
- 1/4 teaspoon salt
- 1 cup buttermilk (or 1 cup milk mixed with 1 tablespoon vinegar or lemon juice, let sit for 5 minutes)
- 1 large egg
- 2 tablespoons unsalted butter, melted
- 1 teaspoon vanilla extract (optional)
- Butter or oil for cooking
- Maple syrup and additional toppings of your choice (e.g., fresh berries, sliced bananas, chocolate chips, or whipped cream)

Instructions:

1. Mix Dry Ingredients:
- In a large mixing bowl, whisk together the flour, sugar, baking powder, baking soda, and salt.
2. Mix Wet Ingredients:
- In a separate bowl, whisk together the buttermilk, egg, melted butter, and vanilla extract (if using).
3. Combine Wet and Dry Ingredients:
- Pour the wet ingredients into the dry ingredients and gently stir until just combined. Be careful not to overmix; a few lumps in the batter are okay.
4. Preheat the Griddle or Pan:
- Place a non-stick griddle or a large skillet over medium- high heat. Add a small amount of butter or oil and let it melt and coat the cooking surface.
5. Ladle and Cook:
- Using a ladle or measuring cup, pour about 1/4 cup of the pancake batter onto the griddle for each pancake. Use the back of the ladle to spread the batter into a round shape if needed.

6. Cook Until Bubbles Form:

· Cook the pancakes for 2-3 minutes or until small bubbles form on the surface.

7. Flip and Cook the Other Side:

· Carefully flip each pancake with a spatula and cook for an additional 2-3 minutes, or until they are golden brown on both sides and cooked through. You may need to adjust the heat if the pancakes are cooking too quickly or slowly.

8. Keep Warm:

· Transfer the cooked pancakes to a warm oven (around 200°F or 93°C) to keep them warm while you cook the remaining batch.

9. Serve:

· Serve your classic pancakes hot with a drizzle of maple syrup and your choice of additional toppings, such as fresh berries, sliced bananas, chocolate chips, or a dollop of whipped cream.

10. Enjoy:

· Enjoy your homemade classic pancakes for a delicious breakfast or brunch treat!

· Feel free to customize your pancakes by adding your favorite ingredients to the batter, such as blueberries, chocolate chips, or chopped nuts. Pancakes are wonderfully versatile and can be tailored to suit your taste preferences.

Greek Yogurt Pancakes

Prep Time: 10 minutes | Cook Time: 10 minutes | Total Time: 20 minutes S

erving Size: Makes approximately 8-10 pancakes

Ingredients:

- 1 cup all-purpose flour
- 2 tablespoons granulated sugar
- 1 teaspoon baking powder
- 1/2 teaspoon baking soda
- 1/4 teaspoon salt
- 1 cup Greek yogurt (plain or flavored)
- 2 large eggs
- 1/4 cup milk (any type)
- 1/2 teaspoon vanilla extract (optional)
- Butter or cooking oil for the pan

Instructions:

1. Mix Dry Ingredients:

- In a mixing bowl, whisk together the flour, sugar, baking powder, baking soda, and salt.

2. Mix Wet Ingredients:

- In another bowl, combine the Greek yogurt, eggs, milk, and vanilla extract (if using). Mix until the ingredients are well combined and smooth.

3. Combine Wet and Dry Ingredients:

- Pour the wet ingredients into the dry ingredients. Stir until just combined. The batter may be thick, but that's okay.

4. Preheat the Skillet:

- Place a non-stick skillet or griddle over medium heat. Add a small amount of butter or cooking oil and let it melt, coating the cooking surface.

5. Cook the Pancakes:

- Scoop a portion of the pancake batter (about 1/4 cup) onto the hot skillet for each pancake. Use the back of a spoon to gently spread the batter into a round shape if needed.

- Cook the pancakes for 2-3 minutes on each side, or until they are golden brown and cooked through. You'll know they're ready to flip when small bubbles form on the surface.

6. Keep Warm:

- Transfer the cooked pancakes to a warm oven (around 200°F or 93°C) to keep them warm while you cook the remaining batch.

7. Serve:

- Serve your Greek Yogurt Pancakes hot with your favorite toppings. Popular options include maple syrup, fresh berries, sliced bananas, chopped nuts, or a dollop of Greek yogurt.

8. Enjoy:

- Enjoy your delicious and protein-packed Greek Yogurt Pancakes for a satisfying breakfast or brunch!

Variations:

- Experiment with different flavors by using flavored Greek yogurt, such as honey or vanilla.

- Add a handful of chocolate chips or blueberries to the pancake batter for a sweet twist.

- For a healthier version, use whole wheat flour or almond flour and top with a drizzle of honey and fresh fruit.

These Greek Yogurt Pancakes are a fantastic way to incorporate extra protein and creaminess into your breakfast routine. Cus- tomize them with your favorite toppings and enjoy a nutritious and delicious start to your day!

French Toast

Prep Time: 10 minutes | Cook Time: 10 minutes | Total Time: 20 minutes

Serving Size: Makes 4-6 slices of French toast

Ingredients:

- 4-6 slices of bread (stale or day-old bread works well)
- 2 large eggs
- 1/2 cup milk
- 1/2 teaspoon vanilla extract
- 1/4 teaspoon ground cinnamon (optional)
- 1/8 teaspoon salt
- Butter or cooking oil for the pan
- Maple syrup, powdered sugar, fresh berries, or other top- pings of your choice

Instructions:

1. Mix the Batter:

- In a mixing bowl, whisk together the eggs, milk, vanilla extract, ground cinnamon (if using), and a pinch of salt. Mix until the ingredients are well combined.

2. Preheat the Griddle or Pan:

- Place a griddle or a large skillet over medium heat and let it warm up. Add a small amount of butter or cooking oil to coat the cooking surface.

3. Dip the Bread:

- Dip each slice of bread into the egg mixture, making sure both sides are soaked but not overly saturated. Allow any excess egg mixture to drip off.

4. Cook the French Toast:

- Place the dipped bread slices on the hot griddle or skillet. Cook for about 2-3 minutes on each side or until they are golden brown and slightly crispy.

5. Keep Warm:

- As each slice of French toast is done, you can keep them warm in a low-temperature oven (around 200°F or 93°C) while you cook the rest.

6. Serve:

- Serve the French toast slices hot with your choice of top- pings. Popular options include maple syrup, powdered sugar, fresh berries, whipped cream, sliced bananas, or a sprinkle of cinnamon.

7. Enjoy:

Enjoy your homemade French toast for a delicious and satisfying breakfast or brunch!

Variations:

·   For extra flavor, you can add a pinch of nutmeg or a dash of orange zest to the egg mixture.

·   Experiment with different types of bread, such as challah, brioche, or whole-grain bread, for unique variations of French toast.

·   Try stuffing your French toast with ingredients like cream cheese and fruit preserves or Nutella and banana slices for a delightful twist. Simply make a sandwich with two slices of dipped bread and cook as usual.

French toast is a versatile and comforting breakfast classic that can be customized to your taste with a variety of toppings and fillings.

Breakfast Burrito

Prep Time: 10 minutes | Cook Time: 10 minutes | Total Time: 20 minutes

Serving Size: 1 breakfast burrito

Ingredients:

- 2 large eggs
- Salt and black pepper, to taste
- 1-2 strips of cooked bacon or cooked sausage links, crum- bled or sliced
- 1/4 cup shredded cheese (cheddar, Monterey Jack, or your favorite)
- 2 tablespoons salsa (mild, medium, or hot, depending on your preference)
- 1 large flour tortilla (burrito-sized)
- Optional toppings: diced tomatoes, diced onions, sliced avocado, sour cream, or chopped cilantro

Instructions:

1. Cook the Eggs:

- In a bowl, crack the eggs and season with a pinch of salt and a dash of black pepper. Beat the eggs until the yolks and whites are well combined.
- Heat a non-stick skillet over medium heat. Add a small amount of butter or cooking oil if needed.
- Pour the beaten eggs into the skillet. Cook and scramble them until they are fully cooked but still slightly moist. Remove from heat.

2. Prepare the Fillings:

- While the eggs are cooking, prepare your choice of break- fast protein (cooked bacon or sausa- ge) and any optional toppings you'd like to add (diced tomatoes, onions, sliced avocado, etc.).

3. Assemble the Burrito:

- Lay a large flour tortilla flat on a clean surface.
- Place the scrambled eggs in the center of the tortilla, leaving some space around the edges.
- Sprinkle the crumbled bacon or sliced sausage over the eggs.
- Add the shredded cheese on top of the eggs and protein.
- Spoon the salsa evenly over the cheese.

4. Roll Up the Burrito:

- To roll up the burrito, first fold in the sides of the tortilla. Then, starting from the bottom, fold it up and over the fillings.

5. Serve and Enjoy:

- Place the breakfast burrito seam side down on a plate.

- If desired, top the burrito with any optional toppings you prepared earlier, such as diced tomatoes, onions, sliced avocado, sour cream, or chopped cilantro.

- Serve your delicious breakfast burrito hot and enjoy!

Variations:

- Customize your breakfast burrito with additional ingredi- ents like sautéed bell peppers, onions, or mushrooms.

- You can also add a touch of heat by including diced jalapeños or hot sauce.

- For a healthier option, consider using whole wheat tortillas and adding spinach or kale to the eggs for added greens.

Mini Breakfast Quesadillas

Prep Time: 10 minutes | Cook Time: 10 minutes | Total Time: 20 minutes

Serving Size: Makes 4 mini quesadillas

Ingredients:

- 4 small flour tortillas (soft taco size)
- 4 large eggs
- Salt and black pepper, to taste
- 1/2 cup shredded cheese (cheddar, Monterey Jack, or your favorite)
- 1/4 cup salsa (mild, medium, or hot, depending on your preference)
- Butter or cooking oil for cooking

Instructions:

1. Prepare the Eggs:

- Crack the eggs into a bowl. Season with a pinch of salt and a dash of black pepper. Beat the eggs until the yolks and whites are well combined.

2. Cook the Eggs:

- Heat a non-stick skillet over medium heat. Add a small amount of butter or cooking oil if needed.
- Pour the beaten eggs into the skillet and cook, stirring gently, until they are scrambled and just set. Remove from heat.

3. Assemble the Quesadillas:

- Lay out the 4 flour tortillas on a clean surface.
- Sprinkle the shredded cheese evenly over two of the tortillas.
- Spoon the scrambled eggs evenly over the cheese.
- Add a dollop of salsa on top of the eggs.
- Place the remaining two tortillas on top of each prepared tortilla to form quesadilla sandwiches.

4. Cook the Quesadillas:

- Heat a clean skillet or griddle over medium-high heat. Place the assembled quesadillas on the hot surface.
- Cook each quesadilla for about 2-3 minutes on each side, or until they are golden brown and crispy, and the cheese is melted.

5. Slice and Serve:

· Remove the cooked quesadillas from the skillet and let them cool for a minute.

· Use a sharp knife or a pizza cutter to slice each quesadilla into halves or quarters.

6. Serve and Enjoy:

· Serve your Mini Breakfast Quesadillas hot and enjoy! They are perfect for dipping in additional salsa or even sour cream if desired.

Variations:

· Customize your mini quesadillas by adding ingredients like diced bell peppers, onions, cooked bacon or sausage, diced tomatoes, or chopped fresh herbs like cilantro.

· If you prefer a spicier kick, consider adding sliced jalapeños or hot sauce to the filling.

These Mini Breakfast Quesadillas are a tasty and portable way to enjoy a flavorful breakfast. They're great for busy mornings or as a snack anytime you're craving a delicious cheesy and eggy treat!

Breakfast Tostada

Ingredients:

- 4 small tostada shells or corn tortillas
- 1 cup refried beans (canned or homemade)
- 1 cup shredded cheddar or Monterey Jack cheese
- 4 large eggs
- 1 ripe avocado, sliced
- 1/2 cup salsa (optional)
- Salt and pepper, to taste
- Chopped fresh cilantro or sliced green onions for garnish (optional)

Instructions:

1. Warm the Tostadas:

- Preheat your oven to 350°F (175°C). Place the tostada shells or corn tortillas directly on the oven rack and warm them for about 5-7 minutes until they become slightly crisp. Alternatively, you can warm them in a dry skillet over medium heat for a few seconds on each side.

2. Prepare the Refried Beans:

- Heat the refried beans in a saucepan over low heat or in the microwave until they are hot and easy to spread. Stir occasionally to prevent sticking.

3. Cook the Eggs:

- In a non-stick skillet, melt a small amount of butter or cooking oil over medium-low heat. Crack the eggs into the skillet, being careful not to break the yolks. Season with a pinch of salt and pepper. Cook the eggs until the whites are set, but the yolks are still slightly runny (about 2-3 minutes). If you prefer over-easy eggs, gently flip them and cook for an additional minute.

4. Assemble the Tostadas:

- Lay out the warm tostada shells on serving plates.
- Spread a generous spoonful of refried beans evenly on each tostada shell.
- Sprinkle shredded cheese over the refried beans while they're still warm, allowing the cheese to melt slightly.

5. Add the Fried Egg:

- Carefully transfer a fried egg onto each tostada, placing it on top of the cheese and beans.

6. Top with Avocado:

· Arrange slices of ripe avocado over the fried eggs.

7. Optional Salsa:

· If you like some extra flavor and a bit of heat, drizzle a spoonful of salsa over the avocado.

8. Garnish and Serve:

· Garnish your breakfast tostadas with chopped fresh cilantro or sliced green onions if desired.

9. Serve Immediately:

· These tostadas are best enjoyed right away while the eggs are still warm and the toppings are fresh.

These Breakfast Tostadas with Refried Beans, Cheese, Fried Egg, and Avocado are a hearty and flavorful way to start your day. Customize them with your favorite toppings or hot sauce for an extra kick of flavor. Enjoy!

Blueberry Muffins

Ingredients:

- 1 1/2 cups all-purpose flour
- 1/2 cup granulated sugar
- 2 teaspoons baking powder
- 1/2 teaspoon baking soda
- 1/2 teaspoon salt
- 1/2 cup (1 stick) unsalted butter, melted and slightly cooled
- 2 large eggs
- 1 cup plain yogurt (or Greek yogurt)
- 1 teaspoon vanilla extract
- 1 1/2 cups fresh or frozen blueberries (if using frozen, do not thaw)
- Zest of 1 lemon (optional)
- Coarse sugar for topping (optional)

Instructions:

1. Preheat the Oven: Preheat your oven to 375°F (190°C). Line a muffin tin with paper liners or grease the muffin cups.

2. Mix Dry Ingredients: In a large mixing bowl, whisk to- gether the flour, granulated sugar, baking powder, baking soda, and salt. If you're using lemon zest for extra flavor, add it to the dry mixture.

3. Combine Wet Ingredients: In a separate bowl, beat the melted butter, eggs, yogurt, and vanilla extract until well combined.

4. Combine Wet and Dry Ingredients: Pour the wet ingre- dients into the dry ingredients and stir gently until just combined. Be careful not to overmix; it's okay if the batter is a bit lumpy.

5. Add Blueberries: Gently fold in the blueberries. If you're using frozen blueberries, they may cause the batter to turn slightly purple, but that's okay.

6. Fill Muffin Cups: Using a spoon or ice cream scoop, fill each muffin cup about 2/3 full with batter.

7. Optional Topping: If desired, sprinkle a pinch of coarse sugar on top of each muffin for a slightly sweet and crunchy finish.

8. Bake: Place the muffin tin in the preheated oven and bake for 18-20 minutes, or until the muffins are golden brown and a toothpick inserted into the center comes out clean.

9. Cool: Allow the muffins to cool in the tin for a few minutes, then transfer them to a wire rack to cool completely.

10. Serve: Once the blueberry muffins have cooled, serve them and enjoy! They're great for breakfast, as a snack, or with a cup of coffee or tea.

Feel free to customize these muffins by adding a streusel top- ping, a drizzle of lemon glaze, or even a handful of chopped nuts. This recipe yields approximately 12 delicious blueberry muffins.

Coffee Cake

Ingredients:

For the Cake:

- 2 cups all-purpose flour
- 1 cup granulated sugar
- 1/2 cup unsalted butter, softened
- 1 cup sour cream
- 2 large eggs
- 1 teaspoon vanilla extract
- 1 teaspoon baking powder
- 1/2 teaspoon baking soda
- 1/4 teaspoon salt

For the Cinnamon Streusel Topping:

- 1/2 cup granulated sugar
- 1/2 cup all-purpose flour
- 1 teaspoon ground cinnamon
- 1/4 cup unsalted butter, cold and cubed

Instructions:

1. Preheat the Oven: Preheat your oven to 350°F (175°C). Grease and flour a 9x9-inch (23x23 cm) square baking pan or a similar-sized baking dish.

2. Prepare the Streusel Topping: In a small bowl, combine the 1/2 cup granulated sugar, 1/2 cup flour, and 1 teaspoon ground cinnamon. Add the cold, cubed butter and use a pastry cutter or your fingers to cut the butter into the dry ingredients until you have a crumbly texture. Set aside.

3. Prepare the Cake Batter: In a large mixing bowl, cream together the softened butter and 1 cup granulated sugar until light and fluffy. Add the eggs, one at a time, mixing well after each addition. Stir in the vanilla extract.

4. Combine Dry Ingredients: In a separate bowl, whisk together the 2 cups all-purpose flour, baking powder, baking soda, and salt.

5. Alternate Mixing: Gradually add the dry ingredients to the butter and sugar mixture, alternating with the sour cream. Begin and end with the dry ingredients. Mix until just combined; do not over-mix.

6. Layer the Batter and Topping: Spread half of the cake batter into the prepared baking pan. Sprinkle half of the cinnamon streusel topping evenly over the batter. Add the remaining batter on top and spread it out, then finish by sprinkling the rest of the streusel topping.

7. Bake: Place the pan in the preheated oven and bake for 35- 40 minutes, or until a toothpick inserted into the center comes out clean, and the cake is golden brown.

8. Cool: Allow the coffee cake to cool in the pan for about 10-15 minutes before transferring it to a wire rack to cool completely.

9. Serve: Once the coffee cake has cooled, slice it into squares or rectangles and serve. Enjoy with a cup of coffee or tea!

This homemade coffee cake is perfect for breakfast, brunch, or as a sweet treat with your favorite warm beverage. The cinnamon streusel topping adds a delightful crumbly texture and a touch of sweetness to the moist cake.

Banana Bread

Ingredients:

- 2 to 3 ripe bananas, mashed (about 1 cup)
- 2/3 cup granulated sugar
- 1/2 cup unsalted butter, softened
- 2 large eggs
- 1 teaspoon vanilla extract
- 1 1/2 cups all-purpose flour
- 1 teaspoon baking soda
- 1/2 teaspoon salt
- 1/2 teaspoon ground cinnamon (optional)
- 1/2 cup chopped nuts (walnuts or pecans, optional)
- 1/2 cup chocolate chips (optional)

Instructions:

1. Preheat the Oven: Preheat your oven to 350°F (175°C). Grease and flour a 9x5-inch (23x13 cm) loaf pan.
2. Mash the Bananas: In a mixing bowl, mash the ripe bananas with a fork until smooth. You can use 2 to 3 bananas depending on their size.
3. Cream Butter and Sugar: In a separate large mixing bowl, cream together the softened butter and granulated sugar until the mixture becomes light and fluffy.
4. Add Eggs and Vanilla: Beat in the eggs one at a time, ensuring each is fully incorporated before adding the next. Stir in the vanilla extract.
5. Combine Dry Ingredients: In another bowl, whisk together the all-purpose flour, baking soda, salt, and ground cinna- mon (if using).
6. Combine Wet and Dry Ingredients: Gradually add the dry ingredients to the banana mixture, stirring until just combined. Be careful not to overmix; a few lumps are okay.
7. Add Optional Ingredients: If you like, fold in the chopped nuts and chocolate chips for extra flavor and texture.
8. Transfer to the Loaf Pan: Pour the banana bread batter into the greased and floured loaf pan, sprea- ding it evenly.
9. Bake: Place the pan in the preheated oven and bake for approximately 60-70 minutes, or until a toothpick or cake tester inserted into the center comes out clean, with no wet batter clinging to it. Baking times may vary slightly, so keep an eye on it.

10. Cool: Allow the banana bread to cool in the pan for about 10- 15 minutes. Then, run a knife around the edges to loosen it, and transfer it to a wire rack to cool completely.

11. Slice and Serve: Once completely cooled, slice the banana bread and serve. Enjoy!

This homemade banana bread is moist, flavorful, and perfect for breakfast, as a snack, or as a sweet treat any time of day. Customize it with your choice of nuts or chocolate chips, or enjoy it as it is.

Lunch Time

Grilled Cheese Sandwich

Prep Time: 5 minutes | Cook Time: 10 minutes | Total Time: 15 minutes

Serving Size: 1 sandwich with soup

Ingredients:

- For the Grilled Cheese Sandwich:
- 2 slices of bread (white, whole wheat, or your choice)
- 2-4 slices of your favorite cheese (cheddar, American, Swiss, etc.)
- 2 tablespoons butter, softened
- Optional add-ins: sliced tomatoes, bacon, or cooked spinach (if desired)

Instructions:

1. Prepare the Grilled Cheese Sandwich:
- Spread one side of each slice of bread with a thin layer of softened butter.
2. Assemble the Sandwich:
- Place the cheese slices between the two slices of bread, buttered sides facing out. If you're adding any optional ingredients like sliced tomatoes, bacon, or cooked spinach, place them between the cheese slices.
3. Grill the Sandwich:
- Heat a skillet or griddle over medium-high heat. Once it's hot, carefully place the assembled sandwich in the skillet.
- Cook the sandwich for about 2-3 minutes on each side, or until the bread is golden brown and the cheese is melted. You can press down on the sandwich gently with a spatula to help it cook evenly.
4. Serve:
- Once the sandwich is golden brown and the cheese is gooey, remove it from the skillet.
- Pour the tomato soup into a bowl or a soup mug.
5. Enjoy:
- Serve your Grilled Cheese Sandwich alongside a bowl of tomato soup.
- Garnish the soup with fresh basil or parsley if desired.

Variations:

- Get creative with your grilled cheese by adding ingredients like caramelized onions, sliced apples, or different types of cheese.
- For a twist on classic tomato soup, you can add a pinch of red pepper flakes for a bit of heat or a dollop of sour cream for extra creaminess.

Grilled Cheese Sandwiches paired with Tomato Soup is a com- forting and timeless combination, perfect for a satisfying and delicious meal. It's a favorite for kids and adults alike!

Italian Grilled Cheese Sandwich with Marinara Dip

Prep Time: Approximately 10 minutes | Cook Time: Approximately 10 minutes

Serving Size: 2 sandwiches

Ingredients:

- For the Grilled Cheese Sandwich:
- 4 slices of Italian or Sourdough bread
- 4 slices of mozzarella cheese
- 4 slices of provolone cheese
- 4 slices of deli ham
- 8 slices of salami
- 8 slices of pepperoni
- 4-6 fresh basil leaves
- 2 tablespoons butter, softened
- Parmesan cheese

For the Marinara Dip:

- 1 cup marinara sauce (store-bought or homemade)

Instructions:

1. Prepare the Marinara Dip:
- If you're using store-bought marinara sauce, heat it in a small saucepan over low heat or in the microwave until warm. If using homemade marinara, warm it up as well.

2. Assemble the Grilled Cheese Sandwich:
- Lay out 4 slices of Italian bread.
- On each of the bottom slices, place a slice of mozzarella cheese, followed by a slice of provolone cheese, and then the meat, and 2-3 fresh basil leaves.
- Top each sandwich with the remaining bread slices to create two sandwiches.

3. Grill the Sandwiches:
- Heat a skillet or griddle over medium heat.
- Spread a thin layer of softened butter on the outside of each sandwich and sprinkle with parmesan cheese
- Place the sandwiches in the skillet and cook for about 3-4 minutes on each side, or until the bread is toasted, and the cheese is melted. You can also use a panini press if you have one.

4. Serve:
- Cut the grilled cheese sandwiches in half diagonally.
- Serve the sandwiches hot with a side of warm marinara sauce for dipping.

Enjoy your delicious Italian grilled cheese sandwiches with marinara dip! This recipe serves 2, making it perfect for a quick lunch or dinner for two people.

Classic Tuna Salad Sandwich Recipe

Prep Time: 10 minutes | Total Time: 10 minutes

Servings: 2 sandwiches

Ingredients:

- 2 cans (5 oz each) of canned tuna, drained
- 1/4 cup mayonnaise
- 1/4 cup diced celery
- 2 tablespoons diced red onion
- 1 tablespoon sweet pickle relish (optional)
- 1 teaspoon Dijon mustard (optional)
- Salt and pepper, to taste
- 4 slices of bread (white, wheat, or your choice)
- Lettuce leaves (optional)
- Sliced tomatoes (optional)

Instructions:

1. Prepare the Tuna Salad:

- In a mixing bowl, combine the drained tuna, diced celery, diced red onion, sweet pickle relish (if using), and Dijon mustard (if using). Mix well to combine all the ingredients.

2. Add Mayonnaise:

- Add the mayonnaise to the tuna mixture. Start with 1/4 cup, and you can adjust the amount to your preferred level of creaminess. Mix until all ingredients are well coated. You can add more mayonnaise if needed.

3. Season with Salt and Pepper:

- Season the tuna salad with salt and pepper to taste. Be mindful of the salt since canned tuna can be salty.

4. Assemble the Sandwiches:

- Lay out four slices of bread. If desired, place a lettuce leaf on two of the slices.
- Divide the tuna salad evenly between the two slices with lettuce.
- If you like, add sliced tomatoes on top of the tuna salad.
- Top with the remaining two slices of bread.

5. Slice and Serve:

· Using a sharp knife, slice each sandwich in half diagonally.

· Serve immediately, or wrap the sandwiches in parchment paper or plastic wrap for a convenient on-the-go meal.

6. Optional Variations:

· Add slices of cheese (cheddar, Swiss, or your choice) to make it a tuna melt. Place the assembled sandwiches in a preheated oven until the cheese is melted and bubbly.

· For a kick of heat, add a pinch of red pepper flakes or a dash of hot sauce to the tuna salad.

· Experiment with different bread types like whole grain, sourdough, or ciabatta.

· Customize your sandwich with your favorite toppings like avocado, pickles, or cucumber slices.

This classic tuna salad sandwich recipe is a quick and satisfying meal that's perfect for lunch or a light dinner. Feel free to adjust the ingredients to suit your taste preferences. Enjoy!

BLT Sandwich (Bacon, Lettuce, and Tomato)

Prep Time: 10 minutes | Cook Time: 10 minutes (for bacon) | Total Time: 20 minutes

Serving Size: 1 sandwich

Ingredients:

- 2 slices of bread (white, whole wheat, sourdough, or your choice)
- 4-6 strips of bacon
- 2-3 lettuce leaves (such as iceberg or Romaine)
- 2-3 slices of ripe tomato
- 1-2 tablespoons mayonnaise
- Salt and black pepper, to taste
- Optional: Dill pickles or avocado slices for extra flavor

Instructions:

1. Cook the Bacon:
- In a skillet over medium heat, cook the bacon until it's crispy and golden brown. This usually takes about 4-5 minutes per side. Drain the cooked bacon on paper towels to remove excess grease.
2. Toast the Bread (Optional):
- If you prefer your BLT with toasted bread, you can lightly toast the slices in a toaster or a toaster oven.
3. Assemble the BLT:
- On one slice of bread, spread a layer of mayonnaise.
- Layer the cooked bacon strips evenly on top of the mayo.
- Place the lettuce leaves on top of the bacon.
- Add the slices of ripe tomato on top of the lettuce.
- If desired, add a pinch of salt and a dash of black pepper to season the tomato slices.
- Optionally, you can add dill pickles or avocado slices for extra flavor and texture.
4. Complete the Sandwich:
- Place the second slice of bread on top of the sandwich to complete it.
5. Slice and Serve:
- Using a sharp knife, cut the BLT sandwich in half diagonally to create two triangular halves.

6. Enjoy:

· Serve your delicious BLT sandwich immediately. It's perfect for a classic and satisfying lunch or a quick and tasty dinner!

7. Variations:

· For a healthier option, you can use turkey bacon or turkey slices instead of traditional bacon.

· Experiment with different types of lettuce or greens, such as arugula or spinach, for a unique flavor and texture.

· Customize your BLT with condiments like mustard or avo- cado mayonnaise for added flavor.

A classic BLT sandwich is a timeless favorite, known for its simple yet delicious combination of crispy bacon, fresh lettuce, and ripe tomatoes. Enjoy it as-is or make it your own by adding your favorite twists and toppings such as avocado or cheese!

Italian Sub Sandwich

Prep Time: 10 minutes | Total Time: 10 minutes

Serving Size: 1 sandwich

Ingredients:

- 1 Italian sub roll or baguette
- 2-3 slices each of Italian cold cuts (such as salami, pepper- oni, and mortadella)
- 2-3 slices of provolone cheese (or your preferred Italian cheese)
- 1/4 cup shredded iceberg lettuce or Romaine lettuce
- 2-3 slices of ripe tomato
- 2-3 slices of red onion (optional)
- 2-3 slices of red bell pepper (optional)
- Sliced black olives (optional)
- Pickled banana pepper rings (optional)
- Salt and black pepper, to taste
- Red wine vinegar and olive oil (optional, for drizzling)
- Italian dressing (optional, for extra flavor)

Instructions:

1. Slice the Bread:

- Slice the Italian sub roll or baguette in half lengthwise, but not all the way through, so you can open it like a book.

2. Layer the Ingredients:

- Start by layering the Italian cold cuts (salami, pepperoni, and mortadella) on the bottom half of the bread.
- Place the provolone cheese slices on top of the cold cuts.
- Add the shredded lettuce, followed by the slices of ripe tomato.
- If desired, layer the red onion slices, red bell pepper slices, black olives, and banana pepper rings on top of the tomato.
- Season with a pinch of salt and a dash of black pepper.

3. Optional Dressing:

- If you prefer, drizzle a bit of red wine vinegar and olive oil over the ingredients for added flavor. Alternatively, you can use Italian dressing for extra zing.

4. Complete the Sandwich:

· Close the sandwich by placing the top half of the bread over the layered ingredients.

5. Slice and Serve:

· Using a sharp knife, cut the Italian sub sandwich in half diagonally to create two triangular halves.

6. Enjoy:

· Serve your Italian Sub Sandwich immediately. It's a delight- ful and savory combination of Italian flavors!

Classic Club Sandwich

Prep Time: 15 minutes | Total Time: 15 minutes

Serving Size: 1 sandwich

Ingredients:

- 3 slices of toasted bread (white, whole wheat, or your choice)
- 2-3 slices of cooked bacon
- 2-3 slices of roasted turkey breast
- 2-3 slices of ham
- 2-3 slices of Swiss or cheddar cheese
- 2 leaves of lettuce (such as iceberg or Romaine)
- 2-3 slices of ripe tomato
- 1-2 tablespoons mayonnaise
- Toothpicks or sandwich picks
- Salt and black pepper, to taste

Instructions:

1. Toast the Bread:

- Toast three slices of bread until they are lightly browned and crispy. You can use a toaster or a toaster oven.

2. Prepare the Fillings:

- Cook the bacon until it's crispy, and then drain it on paper towels to remove excess grease.
- Gather the roasted turkey breast, ham, Swiss or cheddar cheese slices, lettuce leaves, and ripe tomato slices.

3. Assemble the Club Sandwich:

- Lay out one slice of toasted bread on a clean surface.
- Spread a thin layer of mayonnaise over the top side of the bread.
- Place one leaf of lettuce on top of the mayonnaise.
- Add the turkey slices on top of the lettuce.
- Place the second slice of toasted bread on top of the turkey.
- Spread mayonnaise on the top side of the second bread slice.
- Layer the ham slices, crispy bacon strips, and Swiss or cheddar cheese slices on top of the mayonnaise.
- Add the second leaf of lettuce and the tomato slices.
- Season the tomato with a pinch of salt and a dash of black pepper.
- Top the sandwich with the third slice of toasted bread, pressing it down gently to hold everything together.

4. Secure with Picks:

· Using toothpicks or sandwich picks, secure the sandwich in quarters or halves. This will make it easier to handle and prevent the layers from sliding apart.

5. Slice and Serve:

· Use a sharp knife to cut the club sandwich diagonally into two triangular halves.

6. Enjoy:

· Serve your classic Club Sandwich immediately. It's a hearty and satisfying combination of flavors and textures!

Variations:

· Customize your Club Sandwich by adding ingredients like avocado slices, sliced hard-boiled egg, or different types of cheese.

· If you like a bit of tanginess, you can spread Dijon mustard or honey mustard on one of the bread slices.

· For a lighter version, you can use turkey bacon and whole wheat bread.

The Club Sandwich is a classic and delicious option for a satisfy- ing meal, whether you're enjoying it for lunch or dinner. Feel free to adjust the ingredients to your preferences to create your perfect Club Sandwich!

Egg Salad Hoagie Sandwich

Prep Time: Approximately 15 minutes

Serving Size: 4 hoagie sandwiches

Ingredients:

- For the Egg Salad:
- 6 hard-boiled eggs, peeled and chopped
- 1/4 cup mayonnaise
- 2 tablespoons Dijon mustard
- 2 green onions, finely chopped
- 1/4 cup celery, finely chopped
- 1/4 cup red bell pepper, finely chopped
- Salt and pepper to taste
- Optional: a pinch of paprika or cayenne pepper for extra flavor

For the Hoagie Sandwich:

- 4 hoagie rolls or sub rolls
- Lettuce leaves
- Tomato slices
- Red onion slices
- Pickles (optional)
- Sliced cheese (e.g., Swiss, cheddar, or provolone) (optional)

Instructions:

1. Prepare the Egg Salad:
- In a mixing bowl, combine the chopped hard-boiled eggs, mayonnaise, Dijon mustard, green onions, celery, and red bell pepper.
2. Mix everything together until well combined.
- Season the egg salad with salt and pepper to taste. You can also add a pinch of paprika or cayenne pepper for a touch of spice if you like.
3. Assemble the Hoagie Sandwich:
- Slice the hoagie rolls in half horizontally, but not all the way through.

- · Place a few lettuce leaves on the bottom half of each roll.
- · Add a generous scoop of the prepared egg salad on top of the lettuce.
- · If desired, add tomato slices, red onion slices, pickles, and sliced cheese on top of the egg salad.
- · Place the top half of the hoagie roll over the fillings to close the sandwich.

4. Serve:

- · Serve the egg salad hoagie sandwiches immediately, or wrap them in parchment paper or foil for a portable meal.

Enjoy your delicious egg salad hoagie sandwich! This recipe yields 4 servings, making it perfect for a family meal or a small gathering.

Classic Cheeseburger

Prep Time: 10 minutes | Cook Time: 10 minutes | Total Time: 20 minutes

Serving Size: 1 cheeseburger

Ingredients:

- 1/2 pound ground beef (80% lean)
- Salt and black pepper, to taste
- 1 burger bun (sesame seed, brioche, or your choice)
- 1 slice of cheese (American, cheddar, Swiss, or your favorite)
- Lettuce leaves
- Sliced tomato
- Sliced onion
- Pickles
- Ketchup and mustard (optional)
- Butter or cooking oil (for toasting the bun)

Instructions:

1. Form the Burger Patty:

- Divide the ground beef into two equal portions. Take one portion and gently shape it into a patty, about 4-5 inches in diameter and slightly larger than the burger bun.

2. Season the Patty:

- Season both sides of the burger patty with a pinch of salt and a dash of black pepper.

3. Preheat the Grill or Skillet:

- Heat a grill or a skillet over medium-high heat. If you're using a skillet, add a small amount of butter or cooking oil to coat the cooking surface.

4. Cook the Burger:

- Place the burger patty on the hot grill or skillet. Cook for about 3-4 minutes on each side for medium-rare to medium doneness. Adjust the cooking time based on your desired level of doneness.
- During the last minute of cooking, add the slice of cheese on top of the patty. Cover the grill or skillet briefly to allow the cheese to melt.

5. Toast the Bun:

- While the burger is cooking, split the burger bun in half and lightly butter the cut sides.

- Toast the buttered sides of the bun on the grill or in the skillet until they are lightly browned and crispy.

6. Assemble the Cheeseburger:

- Place the cooked cheeseburger patty on the bottom half of the toasted bun.

- Add lettuce leaves, sliced tomato, sliced onion, and pickles on top of the patty.

- If desired, spread ketchup and mustard on the top half of the toasted bun.

7. Complete the Burger:

- Place the top half of the bun with condiments on top of the assembled ingredients to complete the cheeseburger.

8. Serve and Enjoy:

- Serve your classic Cheeseburger hot and enjoy the perfect combination of savory beef, melted cheese, and fresh top- pings!

Variations:

- Customize your cheeseburger with additional toppings like bacon, sautéed mushrooms, avocado slices, or a fried egg.

- Use different types of cheese to create unique flavor profiles.

- If you prefer a meatless option, you can use a plant-based burger patty instead of ground beef.

- Experiment with various sauces and condiments to suit your taste, such as barbecue sauce or sriracha mayo.

Shrimp Po' Boy Sandwich Recipe

Ingredients:

For the Shrimp:

- 1 pound large shrimp, peeled and deveined
- 1 cup buttermilk
- 1 cup all-purpose flour
- 1 teaspoon paprika
- 1/2 teaspoon garlic powder
- 1/2 teaspoon onion powder
- 1/4 teaspoon cayenne pepper (adjust for spiciness)
- Salt and black pepper, to taste
- Vegetable oil, for frying For the Remoulade Sauce:
- 1/2 cup mayonnaise
- 2 tablespoons Dijon mustard
- 1 tablespoon Creole or whole-grain mustard
- 1 clove garlic, minced
- 1 tablespoon hot sauce (adjust to taste)
- 1 tablespoon lemon juice
- 1 teaspoon paprika
- 1/2 teaspoon cayenne pepper (adjust to taste)
- Salt and black pepper, to taste

For Assembling:

- 4 baguette-style rolls or French bread, split and lightly toasted
- Lettuce leaves
- Sliced tomatoes
- Sliced pickles (optional)
- Sliced red onion (optional)

Instructions:

1. Marinate the Shrimp:

- In a bowl, combine the peeled and deveined shrimp with the buttermilk. Let them soak in the buttermilk for about 30 minutes to an hour. This helps tenderize the shrimp and adds flavor.

2. Prepare the Remoulade Sauce:

- In a separate bowl, whisk together the mayonnaise, Dijon mustard, Creole or whole-grain mustard, minced garlic, hot sauce, lemon juice, paprika, cayenne pepper, salt, and black pepper. Taste and adjust the seasonings and spiciness to your preference. Refrigerate the remoulade sauce until you're ready to assemble the sandwiches.

3. Dredge and Fry the Shrimp:

- In a shallow dish, combine the all-purpose flour, paprika, garlic powder, onion powder, cayenne pepper, salt, and black pepper.

- Remove the shrimp from the buttermilk and let any excess drip off.

- Dredge each shrimp in the seasoned flour mixture, ensuring they are well coated. Shake off any excess flour.

- In a large skillet or deep fryer, heat vegetable oil to 350°F (175°C). Carefully add the coated shrimp in batches, making sure not to overcrowd the pan. Fry for about 2-3 minutes per side, or until the shrimp are golden brown and crispy. Remove with a slotted spoon and place them on a paper towel-lined plate to drain any excess oil.

4. Assemble the Po' Boy Sandwiches:

- Spread a generous amount of the prepared remoulade sauce on the toasted baguette rolls.

- Layer with lettuce leaves, sliced tomatoes, crispy fried shrimp, and any optional toppings like sliced pickles or red onion.

- Close the sandwiches and serve immediately.

5. Enjoy:

- Serve your Shrimp Po' Boy Sandwiches while they're still warm and crispy. They're a delicious taste of New Orleans with a perfect balance of crunchy shrimp, creamy sauce, and fresh toppings.

Greek Turkey Meatball Pita

Ingredients:

For the Turkey Meatballs:

- 1 pound ground turkey
- 1/2 cup breadcrumbs
- 1/4 cup Feta cheese
- 1/4 cup finely chopped onion
- 2 cloves garlic, minced
- 1/4 cup fresh dill, chopped
- 1 teaspoon dried oregano
- Salt and pepper to taste
- Olive oil for cooking

For the Feta Sauce:

- 1/2 cup crumbled feta cheese
- 1/2 cup Greek yogurt
- 1 tablespoon lemon juice
- 1 clove garlic, minced
- Salt and pepper to taste

For the Veggie Toppings:

- 1 cucumber, thinly sliced
- 1 cup cherry tomatoes, halved
- 1/2 red onion, thinly sliced
- 1/2 cup Kalamata olives, pitted and sliced
- Fresh lettuce leaves

For Assembling:

- Pita bread or flatbreads

Instructions:

1. Preheat your oven to 375°F (190°C).

2. In a large mixing bowl, combine ground turkey, bread- crumbs, Feta cheese, chopped onion, minced garlic, chopped dill, dried oregano, salt, and pepper. Mix until all the ingredients are well combined.

3. Shape the mixture into meatballs, about 1 to 1.5 inches in diameter.

4. Heat a skillet over medium-high heat and add a little olive oil. Once the oil is hot, add the turkey meatballs and cook until browned on all sides and cooked through, which should take about 8-10 minutes. Transfer the cooked meatballs to a plate and set aside.

5. In the same skillet, add a bit more olive oil if needed and sauté the sliced red onion until it becomes slightly softened and translucent, about 2-3 minutes. Remove from heat.

6. In a small bowl, prepare the feta sauce by mixing together crumbled feta cheese, Greek yogurt, lemon juice, minced garlic, salt, and pepper. Stir until smooth and creamy.

7. Warm the pita bread or flatbreads in the oven for a few minutes until they are pliable.

8. To assemble each pita wrap, spread a generous spoonful of the feta sauce onto the warmed pita.

9. Add lettuce leaves, cucumber slices, cherry tomatoes, sautéed red onions, and Kalamata olives on top of the feta sauce.

10. Place the turkey meatballs on the veggies.

11. Fold the sides of the pita in and then roll it up tightly to create a wrap.

12. Serve your turkey meatball pita wraps immediately, and enjoy!

Feel free to customize your wraps with additional toppings or herbs according to your preference. These wraps make for a delicious and satisfying meal that's perfect for lunch or dinner.

Creamy Tomato Soup

Prep Time: 10 minutes | Cook Time: 25 minutes | Total Time: 35 minutes

Serving Size: 4 servings

Ingredients:

- For the Tomato Soup:
- 2 tablespoons butter
- 1 onion, finely chopped
- 2 cloves garlic, minced
- 2 (14-ounce) cans of diced tomatoes (fire-roasted for extra flavor, if available)
- 1 (14-ounce) can of tomato sauce
- 2 cups chicken or vegetable broth
- 1 teaspoon dried basil
- 1 teaspoon dried oregano
- 1/2 teaspoon dried thyme
- 1/2 teaspoon sugar
- Salt and black pepper, to taste
- 1/2 cup heavy cream (optional, for creaminess)
- Fresh basil or parsley (for garnish)

Instructions:

1. Prepare the Tomato Soup:

- In a large pot, melt the butter over medium heat. Add the chopped onion and minced garlic. Sauté for about 3- 4 minutes, or until the onions become translucent and fragrant.
- Stir in the diced tomatoes, tomato sauce, chicken or veg- etable broth, dried basil, dried oregano, dried thyme, sugar, salt, and black pepper.
- Bring the mixture to a boil, then reduce the heat to low, cover, and simmer for 15-20 minutes, allowing the flavors to meld together.
- If you prefer a creamy tomato soup, stir in the heavy cream and heat for an additional 2-3 minutes. Adjust the seasoning with more salt and pepper if needed.

2. Serve and Enjoy:

- Ladle the creamy tomato soup into bowls and garnish with fresh basil or parsley if desired.

- Serve each bowl of tomato soup with a warm and crispy Grilled Cheese Sandwich using the recipe above on the side for a comforting and classic combination.

3. Variations:

- Customize your tomato soup by adding a pinch of red pepper flakes for a bit of heat or a drizzle of olive oil for extra richness.

- Creamy Tomato Soup paired with Grilled Cheese Sandwiches is a timeless and satisfying meal, perfect for cozy lunches or comforting dinners. Enjoy the delicious interplay of flavors and textures!

Homemade Chicken Noodle Soup

Prep Time: 15 minutes | Cook Time: 45 minutes | Total Time: 1 hour

Serving Size: 4-6 servings

Ingredients:

- 1 tablespoon olive oil
- 1 medium onion, chopped
- 2 carrots, peeled and sliced
- 2 celery stalks, sliced
- 3 cloves garlic, minced
- 8 cups chicken broth (homemade or store-bought)
- 2 boneless, skinless chicken breasts or 2 cups shredded cooked chicken
- 2 bay leaves
- 1 teaspoon dried thyme
- 1 teaspoon dried rosemary
- Salt and black pepper, to taste
- 2 cups egg noodles (or your favorite pasta)
- 1 cup frozen peas
- Fresh parsley, chopped (for garnish, optional)
- Lemon wedges (for serving, optional)

Instructions:

1. Sauté the Vegetables:

- In a large soup pot or Dutch oven, heat the olive oil over medium heat. Add the chopped onion, sliced carrots, and sliced celery. Sauté for about 5 minutes, or until the vegeta- bles start to soften.
- Add the minced garlic and cook for another 1-2 minutes until fragrant.

2. Add the Broth and Chicken:

- Pour in the chicken broth and add the boneless, skinless chicken breasts (if using uncooked chicken). If using pre- cooked chicken, you can skip this step.
- Add the bay leaves, dried thyme, dried rosemary, salt, and black pepper to the pot. Stir to combine.

3. Simmer the Soup:

- Bring the soup to a boil, then reduce the heat to low. Cover and simmer for about 20-25 minutes, or until the chicken is cooked through (if using uncooked chicken) and the vegetables are tender.

4. Cook the Noodles:

- While the soup is simmering, cook the egg noodles (or your preferred pasta) according to the package instructions until al dente. Drain and set aside.

5. Shred the Chicken:

- If you used uncooked chicken, remove the chicken breasts from the soup and shred them using two forks. Return the shredded chicken to the pot.

6. Add Noodles and Peas:

- Stir in the cooked and drained noodles and the frozen peas. Cook for an additional 5-7 minutes, or until the peas are heated through.

7. Adjust Seasoning:

- Taste the soup and adjust the seasoning with more salt and black pepper if needed.

8. Serve:

- Ladle the homemade Chicken Noodle Soup into bowls, garnish with chopped fresh parsley (if desired), and serve hot.

9. Optional: Lemon Wedges

- For an extra burst of flavor, serve each bowl with a lemon wedge. Squeezing a bit of lemon juice into the soup just before eating adds a refreshing twist.

10. Enjoy:

- Enjoy your comforting and hearty bowl of homemade Chicken Noodle Soup, perfect for warming up on a chilly day or when you're feeling under the weather.

Variations:

- Customize your soup by adding diced potatoes, corn, or green beans for extra vegetables.

- Feel free to use other herbs like fresh thyme or dill for a different flavor profile.

- If you prefer a thicker soup, you can add a slurry of corn- starch and water to thicken the broth. Simply mix 2 table- spoons of cornstarch with 2 tablespoons of water, then stir it into the simmering soup until it thickens.

- For a lower-carb option, you can substitute zucchini noodles or cauliflower rice for the egg noodles.

- Homemade Chicken Noodle Soup is a classic comfort food that warms the soul. It's versatile and can be adjusted to suit your taste preferences or dietary needs. Enjoy!

Homemade Navy Bean Soup

Prep Time: 10 minutes Cook Time: 1 hour 30 minutes Total Time: 1 hour 40 minutes Serving Size: 6-8 servings

Ingredients:

- 1 pound dried navy beans
- 2 tablespoons olive oil
- 1 onion, chopped
- 2 carrots, peeled and diced
- 2 celery stalks, diced
- 3 cloves garlic, minced
- 8 cups water or low-sodium chicken or vegetable broth
- 1 bay leaf
- 1 teaspoon dried thyme
- 1 teaspoon dried rosemary
- 1 teaspoon dried oregano
- 1 teaspoon paprika
- Salt and black pepper, to taste
- 1 ham hock (optional, for extra flavor)
- 2 cups diced ham (optional)
- Fresh parsley, chopped (for garnish, optional)

Instructions:

1. Prepare the Navy Beans:

- Rinse the dried navy beans in a colander under cold running water. Remove any debris or stones.
- In a large bowl, cover the beans with enough water to submerge them by a couple of inches. Let them soak for at least 4 hours or overnight. Drain and rinse before using.

2. Sauté the Vegetables:

- In a large soup pot or Dutch oven, heat the olive oil over medium heat. Add the chopped onion, diced carrots, and diced celery. Sauté for about 5 minutes, or until the vegeta- bles start to soften.
- Add the minced garlic and cook for another 1-2 minutes until fragrant.

3. Add the Beans and Liquid:

- Add the soaked and drained navy beans to the pot with the sautéed vegetables.

- Pour in the water or broth and stir to combine.

4. Season the Soup:

- Add the bay leaf, dried thyme, dried rosemary, dried oregano, paprika, salt, and black pepper to the pot. Stir well.

- If using a ham hock for extra flavor, add it to the pot at this stage.

5. Simmer the Soup:

- Bring the soup to a boil, then reduce the heat to low. Cover and simmer for about 1 hour to 1 hour and 30 minutes, or until the beans are tender and the soup has thickened. Stir occasionally.

6. Optional Ham Addition:

- If you're using diced ham, add it to the soup during the last 15-20 minutes of cooking. This will allow the ham to heat through and infuse its flavor into the soup.

7. Remove the Ham Hock and Bay Leaf:

- If you used a ham hock, remove it from the soup. Discard the bay leaf as well.

8. Adjust Seasoning:

- Taste the soup and adjust the seasoning with more salt and black pepper if needed.

9. Serve:

- Ladle the homemade Navy Bean Soup into bowls, garnish with chopped fresh parsley (if desired), and serve hot.

Variations:

- Customize your navy bean soup by adding diced potatoes, diced tomatoes, or spinach for extra flavor and nutrition.

- For a vegetarian version, omit the ham hock and diced ham, and use vegetable broth instead of chicken broth.

- If you prefer a creamier soup, you can blend a portion of the soup with an immersion blender and then mix it back into the pot.

- Serve the soup with a side of crusty bread or cornbread for a complete meal.

Homemade Navy Bean Soup is a hearty and nutritious dish that's perfect for chilly days. It's rich in flavor and can be tailored to suit your taste preferences. Enjoy!

Italian Wedding Soup

Prep Time: 20 minutes | Cook Time: 30 minutes | Total Time: 50 minutes

Serving Size: 4-6 servings

Ingredients:

- For the Meatballs:
- ½ pound ground beef or ground pork (or a mixture of both)
- ¼ cup breadcrumbs
- ¼ cup grated Parmesan cheese
- ¼ cup chopped fresh parsley
- 1 egg
- 1 clove garlic, minced
- Salt and black pepper, to taste

For the Soup:

- 2 tablespoons olive oil
- 1 onion, chopped
- 2 carrots, peeled and diced
- 2 celery stalks, diced
- 3 cloves garlic, minced
- 8 cups chicken broth (homemade or store-bought)
- 1 cup acini di pepe pasta (or any small pasta of your choice)
- 4 cups fresh spinach or kale, chopped
- Salt and black pepper, to taste
- 1/4 cup grated Parmesan cheese (for serving)

Instructions:

1. Prepare the Meatballs:

- In a mixing bowl, combine the ground beef (or pork), bread- crumbs, grated Parmesan cheese, chopped fresh parsley, egg, minced garlic, salt, and black pepper. Mix until well combined.

- Shape the mixture into small meatballs, about 1 inch in diameter. You should have approximately 24 meatballs. Place them on a baking sheet or plate.

2. Sauté the Vegetables:

- In a large soup pot or Dutch oven, heat the olive oil over medium heat. Add the chopped onion, diced carrots, and diced celery. Sauté for about 5 minutes, or until the vegeta- bles start to soften.

- Add the minced garlic and cook for another 1-2 minutes until fragrant.

3. Add the Broth and Meatballs:

- Pour in the chicken broth and bring it to a boil.

- Carefully add the meatballs to the boiling broth. Reduce the heat to low, cover, and simmer for about 15-20 minutes, or until the meatballs are cooked through.

4. Cook the Pasta:

- While the meatballs are simmering, cook the acini di pepe pasta (or your chosen small pasta) according to the package instructions until al dente. Drain and set aside.

5. Add Spinach or Kale:

- Stir in the chopped fresh spinach or kale into the simmering soup. Cook for an additional 3-5 minu- tes until the greens are wilted.

6. Adjust Seasoning:

- Taste the soup and adjust the seasoning with more salt and black pepper if needed.

7. Serve:

- Ladle the Italian Wedding Soup into bowls, add a portion of cooked pasta to each bowl, and garnish with grated Parmesan cheese.

8. Enjoy:

- Serve your homemade Italian Wedding Soup hot. It's a comforting and hearty soup perfect for any occasion!

Variations:

- Customize your Italian Wedding Soup by using ground turkey or chicken instead of beef or pork for the meatballs.

- Add a squeeze of fresh lemon juice just before serving for a zesty twist.

- Experiment with different greens like escarole or Swiss chard for unique flavors and textures.

Italian Wedding Soup is a delicious and satisfying dish, named for the "marriage" of flavors between the meatballs and greens. Enjoy this comforting soup with a side of crusty bread for a complete meal.

Beef Minestrone Soup

Prep Time: 15 minutes | Cook Time: 1 hour 30 minutes | Total Time: 1 hour 45 minutes

Serving Size: 6-8 servings

Ingredients:

- 1 pound lean ground beef
- 1 onion, chopped
- 2 carrots, peeled and diced
- 2 celery stalks, diced
- 3 cloves garlic, minced
- 1 can (14 ounces) diced tomatoes
- 1 can (14 ounces) crushed tomatoes
- 8 cups beef broth (homemade or store-bought)
- 2 bay leaves
- 1 teaspoon dried oregano
- 1 teaspoon dried basil
- 1/2 teaspoon dried thyme
- Salt and black pepper, to taste
- 1 cup small pasta (such as ditalini, macaroni, or small shells)
- 2 cups chopped fresh spinach or kale
- 1 can (15 ounces) kidney beans, drained and rinsed
- 1/2 cup grated Parmesan cheese (for serving)
- Fresh basil or parsley (for garnish, optional)

Instructions:

1. Brown the Ground Beef:

- In a large soup pot or Dutch oven, cook the lean ground beef over medium-high heat until it's browned and no longer pink, breaking it up into crumbles as it cooks. Drain any excess fat.

2. Sauté the Vegetables:

- Add the chopped onion, diced carrots, and diced celery to the pot with the browned beef. Sauté for about 5 minutes, or until the vegetables start to soften.

- Stir in the minced garlic and cook for another 1-2 minutes until fragrant.

3. Add Tomatoes and Broth:

- Pour in the diced tomatoes, crushed tomatoes, beef broth, bay leaves, dried oregano, dried basil, dried thyme, salt, and black pepper. Stir to combine.

4. Simmer the Soup:

- Bring the soup to a boil, then reduce the heat to low. Cover and simmer for about 45 minutes to 1 hour, allowing the flavors to meld together.

5. Cook the Pasta:

- While the soup is simmering, cook the small pasta according to the package instructions until al dente. Drain and set aside.

6. Add Greens and Beans:

- Stir in the chopped fresh spinach or kale and the drained and rinsed kidney beans. Cook for an additional 5-7 minutes, or until the greens are wilted and the beans are heated through.

7. Adjust Seasoning:

- Taste the soup and adjust the seasoning with more salt and black pepper if needed.

8. Serve:

- To serve, ladle the Beef Minestrone Soup into bowls, add a portion of cooked pasta to each bowl, and garnish with grated Parmesan cheese.

9. Optional: Garnish with Fresh Herbs:

- Optionally, you can garnish each bowl with fresh basil or parsley for an extra burst of flavor.

10. Enjoy:

- Serve your homemade Beef Minestrone Soup hot. It's a hearty and flavorful meal perfect for a satisfying lunch or dinner!

Variations:

- Customize your Beef Minestrone Soup by adding other vegetables like zucchini, green beans, or corn.
- For a spicy twist, you can add a pinch of red pepper flakes or a dash of hot sauce.
- Substitute ground beef with ground turkey or ground chicken for a lighter version of the soup.

Beef Minestrone Soup is a comforting and nutritious dish that's packed with delicious flavors. Enjoy this hearty soup with a side of crusty bread or a simple salad.

Garden Salad

Prep Time: 15 minutes | Total Time: 15 minutes

Serving Size: 4 servings

Ingredients:

For the Salad:

- 6 cups mixed salad greens (e.g., Romaine, iceberg, spinach, arugula)
- 1 cup cherry tomatoes, halved
- 1 cucumber, sliced
- 1 bell pepper, thinly sliced
- 1/2 red onion, thinly sliced
- 1/2 cup sliced black olives (optional)
- 1/4 cup crumbled feta cheese (optional)
- 1/4 cup croutons (optional)
- 1/4 cup fresh basil leaves (for garnish, optional)

For the Dressing:

- 1/4 cup extra-virgin olive oil
- 2 tablespoons balsamic vinegar
- 1 teaspoon Dijon mustard
- 1 clove garlic, minced (optional)
- Salt and black pepper, to taste

1. Instructions:
- Prepare the Dressing (or your favorite store bought dressing):
- In a small bowl, whisk together the extra-virgin olive oil, balsamic vinegar, Dijon mustard, minced garlic (if using), salt, and black pepper until well combined. Taste and adjust the seasoning if needed. Set aside.
2. Assemble the Salad:
- In a large salad bowl, arrange the mixed salad greens as the base.
- Top the greens with cherry tomatoes, cucumber slices, bell pepper slices, thinly sliced red onion, and sliced black olives (if using).

- If desired, sprinkle crumbled feta cheese and croutons over the salad for extra flavor and texture.

3. Serve:

- Drizzle the dressing over the Garden Salad.
- Garnish with fresh basil leaves (if using) for a pop of color and an extra layer of freshness.
- Toss the salad gently just before serving to evenly distribute the dressing and toppings.
- Serve your Garden Salad immediately as a refreshing and nutritious side dish or a light meal.

Variations:

- Customize your Garden Salad with additional vegetables like carrots, radishes, or celery.
- Add protein by including grilled chicken, shrimp, or tofu.
- Experiment with different types of cheese, such as goat cheese or Parmesan.
- For a crunchy twist, try roasted nuts or seeds like almonds or sunflower seeds.
- Swap the dressing for your favorite vinaigrette or a creamy ranch dressing.

This Garden Salad is a versatile and vibrant dish that's perfect for any occasion. Enjoy the freshness of garden-fresh vegetables with your choice of delicious toppings and dressing!

Chicken Caesar Salad

Prep Time: 15 minutes | Cook Time: 15 minutes (for chicken, if not using pre-cooked) | Total Time: 30 minutes

Serving Size: 2-4 servings

Ingredients:

For the Chicken:

- 2 boneless, skinless chicken breasts
- 1 tablespoon olive oil
- Salt and black pepper, to taste
- 1 teaspoon dried oregano (optional)

For the Caesar Dressing:

- 1/2 cup mayonnaise
- 2 cloves garlic, minced
- 2 tablespoons grated Parmesan cheese
- 1 tablespoon Dijon mustard
- 1 tablespoon fresh lemon juice
- 1 teaspoon Worcestershire sauce
- Salt and black pepper, to taste

For the Salad:

- 1 head of Romaine lettuce, washed and chopped
- 1 cup croutons
- 1/4 cup grated Parmesan cheese
- Freshly ground black pepper, to taste
- Lemon wedges (for garnish, optional)

Instructions:

1. Cook the Chicken:
- If using pre-cooked chicken or rotisserie chicken, skip this step. Otherwise, season the chicken breasts with salt, black pepper, and dried oregano (if desired).

- In a skillet or on a grill, heat the olive oil over medium-high heat. Cook the chicken breasts for about 6-7 minutes per side, or until they are no longer pink in the center and have an internal temperature of 165°F (74°C).

- Remove the chicken from heat and let it rest for a few minutes. Slice the cooked chicken into thin strips.

2. Prepare the Caesar Dressing (or use store bought):

- In a bowl, whisk together the mayonnaise, minced garlic, grated Parmesan cheese, Dijon mustard, fresh lemon juice, Worcestershire sauce, salt, and black pepper until well combined. Adjust the seasoning to taste.

3. Assemble the Salad:

- In a large salad bowl, add the chopped Romaine lettuce.

- Drizzle the Caesar dressing over the lettuce, tossing to coat the leaves evenly.

- Add the sliced chicken on top of the dressed lettuce.

- Sprinkle croutons and grated Parmesan cheese over the salad.

- Finish with a dash of freshly ground black pepper and, if desired, a squeeze of fresh lemon juice for extra zing.

4. Serve:

- Divide the Chicken Caesar Salad onto individual plates or serve it family-style in a large bowl.

- Garnish with lemon wedges if you like, and enjoy your delicious and classic Chicken Caesar Salad!

Variations:

- Add bacon bits or crispy prosciutto for extra flavor and texture.

- Include cherry tomatoes, cucumber slices, or roasted red peppers for additional vegetables.

- Top the salad with shaved Parmesan or Pecorino Romano cheese for a gourmet touch.

- For a healthier version, you can use Greek yogurt or a light mayonnaise in the dressing.

Chicken Caesar Salad is a timeless and satisfying dish that's perfect for lunch or dinner. It's versatile, allowing you to customize it with your favorite ingredients and enjoy the classic flavors of Caesar dressing and grilled chicken.

Chinese Chicken Salad

Prep Time: 15 minutes | Cook Time: 10 minutes (for chicken, if not using pre-cooked) | Total Time: 25 minutes

Serving Size: 4 servings

Ingredients:

For the Salad:

- 2 boneless, skinless chicken breasts (or use pre-cooked chicken strips)
- Salt and black pepper, to taste (if cooking chicken)
- 1 tablespoon vegetable oil (if cooking chicken)
- 1 head of iceberg lettuce, chopped
- 1 cup shredded cabbage (green or purple)
- 1 cup shredded carrots
- 1/2 cup sliced green onions
- 1/4 cup sliced almonds, toasted
- 1/4 cup crispy chow mein noodles (optional, for crunch)
- Sesame seeds (for garnish, optional)

For the Dressing (or use your favorite store bought Asian dressing):

- 1/4 cup soy sauce
- 3 tablespoons rice vinegar
- 2 tablespoons sesame oil
- 2 tablespoons honey or brown sugar
- 1 teaspoon grated fresh ginger (or use 1/4 teaspoon ground ginger)
- 1 clove garlic, minced (or use 1/4 teaspoon garlic powder)
- Salt and black pepper, to taste

Instructions:

1. Cook the Chicken (Optional):

- If using pre-cooked chicken strips or leftover chicken, skip this step. Otherwise, follow these simple instructions for cooking chicken breasts:
- Season the chicken breasts with a pinch of salt and black pepper.
- In a skillet, heat 1 tablespoon of vegetable oil over medium- high heat.
- Cook the chicken breasts for about 6-7 minutes per side, or until they're no longer pink inside and reach an internal temperature of 165°F (74°C).
- Remove the chicken from heat and let it rest for a few minutes. Slice the cooked chicken into thin strips.

2. Prepare the Dressing:

- In a small bowl, whisk together 1/4 cup soy sauce, 3 table- spoons rice vinegar, 2 tablespoons sesame oil, 2 tablespoons honey (or brown sugar), grated fresh ginger (or ground ginger), minced garlic (or garlic powder), a pinch of salt, and a dash of black pepper. Mix until well combined. Taste and adjust the seasoning if needed.

3. Assemble the Salad:

· In a large salad bowl, combine the chopped iceberg lettuce, shredded cabbage, shredded carrots, sliced green onions, and toasted sliced almonds.

4. Toss with the Dressing:

· Drizzle the dressing over the salad. Start with a portion of the dressing and add more as desired.

· Toss everything together to evenly coat the salad ingredi- ents with the dressing.

5. Add Chicken and Crunchy Toppings:

· Place the sliced chicken on top of the dressed salad.

· If you're using crispy chow mein noodles, sprinkle them over the salad for extra crunch.

6. Garnish and Serve:

· Optionally, garnish the Chinese Chicken Salad with sesame seeds for a nice finishing touch.

· Serve your delicious and flavorful Chinese Chicken Salad immediately.

Variations:

· Add mandarin orange segments or sliced water chestnuts for extra texture and flavor.

· Use other proteins like cooked shrimp or tofu for a different twist.

· Customize the dressing by adjusting the sweet and savory elements to your taste.

· Experiment with different crunchy toppings like crushed peanuts or cashews.

This Chinese Chicken Salad is a refreshing and satisfying dish that's perfect for a light and tasty meal. Enjoy the combination of crispy vegetables, tender chicken, and flavorful dressing!

Classic Cobb Salad

Prep Time: 20 minutes | Total Time: 20 minutes

Serving Size: 4 servings

Ingredients:

For the Salad:

- 6 cups chopped Romaine lettuce
- 2 cups cooked and diced chicken breast
- 6 strips bacon, cooked and crumbled
- 2 hard-boiled eggs, chopped
- 1 cup cherry tomatoes, halved
- 1 cup diced cucumber
- 1/2 cup crumbled blue cheese or your favorite cheese
- 1 avocado, diced
- 2 tablespoons chopped fresh chives (for garnish, optional) For the Dressing (or your favorite store bought dressing):
- 1/4 cup olive oil
- 2 tablespoons red wine vinegar
- 1 teaspoon Dijon mustard
- 1 clove garlic, minced
- Salt and black pepper, to taste

Instructions:

1. Prepare the Dressing:
- In a small bowl, whisk together the olive oil, red wine vinegar, Dijon mustard, minced garlic, salt, and black pepper until well combined. Set aside.
2. Assemble the Salad:
- In a large salad bowl or on individual serving plates, arrange the chopped Romaine lettuce as the base.
- Arrange the diced chicken breast, crumbled bacon, chopped hard-boiled eggs, cherry tomatoes, diced cucumber, crum- bled blue cheese, and diced avocado in rows on top of the lettuce.
3. Serve:
- Drizzle the dressing over the Cobb Salad.

- If desired, garnish with chopped fresh chives for a burst of flavor and color.
- Serve immediately and enjoy your Classic Cobb Salad!

Variations:

- Feel free to customize your Cobb Salad with your favorite ingredients. Some popular additions include black olives, bell peppers, red onion, or roasted corn.
- Swap the protein by using grilled shrimp, turkey, or even tofu for a different twist.
- Use your preferred cheese, such as feta or cheddar, if you're not a fan of blue cheese.
- For a creamier dressing, you can mix in 2-3 tablespoons of sour cream or Greek yogurt.

Classic Cobb Salad is a hearty and satisfying dish that's perfect for a light meal or a hearty appetizer. Enjoy the combination of fresh vegetables, protein, and a flavorful dressing!

Greek Salad

Prep Time: 15 minutes | Total Time: 15 minutes

Serving Size: 4 servings

Ingredients:

For the Salad:

- 4 cups chopped Romaine lettuce or mixed salad greens
- 2 cups diced tomatoes
- 1 cucumber, sliced
- 1/2 red onion, thinly sliced
- 1 cup Kalamata olives, pitted
- 1 cup crumbled feta cheese
- 1/2 cup chopped fresh parsley (for garnish, optional)

For the Dressing (or your favorite store bought vinaigrette dressing):

- 1/4 cup extra-virgin olive oil
- 2 tablespoons red wine vinegar
- 1 teaspoon dried oregano
- 1 clove garlic, minced
- Salt and black pepper, to taste

Instructions:

1. Prepare the Dressing:
- In a small bowl, whisk together the extra-virgin olive oil, red wine vinegar, dried oregano, minced garlic, salt, and black pepper until well combined. Taste and adjust the seasoning if needed. Set aside.
2. Assemble the Salad:
- In a large salad bowl, arrange the chopped Romaine lettuce or mixed salad greens as the base.
- Top the greens with diced tomatoes, cucumber slices, thinly sliced red onion, Kalamata olives, and crumbled feta cheese.
3. Serve:
- Drizzle the dressing over the Greek Salad.
- If desired, garnish with chopped fresh parsley for an extra burst of freshness and color.
- Toss the salad gently just before serving to evenly distribute the dressing and toppings.

- Serve your Greek Salad immediately as a refreshing and flavorful side dish or a light meal.

Variations:

- Customize your Greek Salad by adding green bell peppers, red bell peppers, or even roasted red peppers.
- Include thinly sliced radishes or artichoke hearts for extra texture and flavor.
- If you prefer a milder cheese, you can use crumbled goat cheese instead of feta.
- For added protein, add grilled chicken, shrimp, or chickpeas.
- If you like a spicier kick, sprinkle some red pepper flakes over the salad.

Greek Salad is a classic and delicious dish that's perfect for any occasion. Enjoy the vibrant flavors of Mediterranean cuisine with this easy-to-make salad!

Appetizers and Snacks

Cheese and Charcuterie Board Recipe

A cheese and charcuterie board is the perfect centerpiece for any gathering, offering a delightful array of flavors and textures. Here's how to create an inviting and well-balanced board:

Ingredients:

Cheeses:
- Soft Cheese: Brie or Camembert
- Hard Cheese: Aged Cheddar or Gouda
- Blue Cheese: Gorgonzola or Roquefort
- Mild Cheese: Havarti or Swiss

Charcuterie:
- Prosciutto
- Salami
- Spanish chorizo
- Pâté or terrine

Accompaniments:
- Mixed nuts: Almonds, walnuts, or pecans
- Fresh fruits: Grapes, apple slices, and berries
- Dried fruits: Apricots or figs
- Olives: A mix of green and black
- Cornichons or pickles

Breads and Crackers:
- Baguette slices
- Artisan crackers
- Breadsticks

Extras:

- Honey or honeycomb
- Fig jam or fruit preserves
- Mustard (for pâté)
- Fresh herbs for garnish (like rosemary or thyme)

Instructions:

1. Choose Your Board: Select a large wooden board or platter for an aesthetically pleasing presentation.
2. Cheese Placement: Start by placing the cheeses on the board. Space them out, and consider cutting some into slices or wedges for easy serving.
3. Add Charcuterie: Fold or roll slices of meats like prosciutto and salami. Arrange them near the cheeses. You can also create small piles or fan them out for visual appeal.
4. Incorporate Breads and Crackers: Fill in gaps with bread and crackers. Offer a variety to pair with different cheeses and meats.
5. Arrange Accompaniments: Scatter nuts, fresh and dried fruits, olives, and cornichons around the board. These not only add color but also offer a palate cleanser between different flavors.
6. Extras for Flavor: Add small bowls or dishes of honey, jams, and mustard to the board. They complement both cheeses and meats wonderfully.
7. Final Touches: Garnish with fresh herbs for a pop of color and freshness.
8. Serving: Provide cheese knives, spreaders, and small forks or toothpicks for easy serving.

Tips:

- Take cheeses out of the fridge about an hour before serving; they're best enjoyed at room temperature.
- Tailor the board to your guests' preferences, considering any dietary restrictions.
- Pair with a selection of wines or craft beers to enhance the flavors.

Enjoy crafting your cheese and charcuterie board, the perfect edible art for any occasion!

Mini Crab Cakes Recipe

Prep Time: 20 minutes | Cook Time: 10 minutes | Total Time: 30 minutes

Serving Size: Makes about 24 mini crab cakes

Ingredients:

Crab Cakes:

- 1 lb lump crab meat, carefully picked over for shells
- 1/4 cup breadcrumbs
- 1/4 cup finely diced bell pepper (red or green)
- 2 green onions, thinly sliced
- 1/4 cup mayonnaise
- 1 egg
- 1 tsp Dijon mustard
- 1 tsp Worcestershire sauce
- 1/2 tsp Old Bay seasoning
- Salt and pepper, to taste
- Lemon zest from 1 lemon

For Coating:

- 1 cup breadcrumbs
- 1/2 tsp paprika

For Frying:

- Vegetable oil

Serving:

- Lemon wedges
- Tartar sauce or remoulade

Instructions:

1. Combine Crab Cake Ingredients: In a large bowl, mix together the crab meat, 1/4 cup breadcrumbs, bell pepper, green onions, mayonnaise, egg, Dijon mustard, Worcestershire sauce, Old Bay seasoning, salt, pepper, and lemon zest. Be gentle to keep the crab pieces intact.

2. Shape the Cakes: Using your hands or a small scoop, form the mixture into small patties, about the size of a golf ball. Flatten them slightly.

3. Coat the Crab Cakes: In a shallow dish, mix 1 cup bread-crumbs with paprika. Coat each crab cake in this bread-crumb mixture.

4. Chill: Place the crab cakes on a baking sheet and chill in the refrigerator for at least 10 minutes. This helps them hold together when cooking.

5. Fry the Crab Cakes: Heat a thin layer of vegetable oil in a large skillet over medium heat. Fry the crab cakes in batches, being careful not to overcrowd the pan. Cook for about 3-4 minutes on each side, or until they are golden brown and crispy.

6. Drain: Remove the crab cakes from the skillet and drain on paper towels.

7. Serve: Serve the mini crab cakes hot with lemon wedges and tartar sauce or remoulade on the side.

Tips:

- If the crab cake mixture seems too loose, you can add a bit more breadcrumbs to help it hold together.

- Make sure the oil is hot before adding the crab cakes to get a nice sear and prevent sticking.

- These crab cakes can also be baked at 375°F for about 12-15 minutes, flipping halfway through, for a lighter version.

These mini crab cakes are a delightful appetizer, packed with the sweet flavor of crab and a crispy breadcrumb coating. They're perfect for parties, as they can be eaten with your fingers and are always a crowd-pleaser.

Bacon-Wrapped Asparagus Recipe

Ingredients:

- 1 bunch of fresh asparagus spears (about 1 pound)
- 6-8 slices of bacon
- Olive oil, for drizzling
- Salt and black pepper, to taste
- Optional: Grated Parmesan cheese or lemon zest for garnish

Instructions:

1. Prep the Asparagus:

- Preheat your oven to 400°F (200°C). Wash the asparagus spears and trim off the tough, woody ends. Pat them dry with a paper towel.

2. Wrap with Bacon:

- Take a slice of bacon and wrap it tightly around one or two asparagus spears, depending on the thickness of the spears. Repeat this process until all the asparagus is wrapped in bacon.

3. Place on a Baking Sheet:

- Line a baking sheet with aluminum foil for easy cleanup. Place the bacon-wrapped asparagus on the baking sheet, making sure the loose end of the bacon is tucked underneath to secure it.

4. Drizzle with Olive Oil and Season:

- Drizzle a little olive oil over the bacon-wrapped asparagus to help with crispiness. Season with a pinch of salt and black pepper.

5. Bake:

- Place the baking sheet in the preheated oven and bake for about 15-20 minutes or until the bacon is crispy and the asparagus is tender. You may want to turn the asparagus halfway through for even cooking.

6. Optional Garnish:

- If desired, you can garnish the bacon-wrapped asparagus with grated Parmesan cheese or a sprinkle of lemon zest for added flavor.

7. Serve:

- Transfer the Bacon-Wrapped Asparagus to a serving platter and enjoy immediately. These make a delicious side dish or appetizer, perfect for any occasion

Stuffed Mushrooms Recipe

Ingredients:

- 12 large white mushrooms
- 1/2 cup Italian-style bread crumbs
- 1/4 cup grated Parmesan cheese
- 2 cloves garlic, minced
- 2 tablespoons fresh parsley, chopped
- 2 tablespoons olive oil
- Salt and black pepper, to taste
- Optional: Red pepper flakes for a touch of spice
- Optional: Fresh basil leaves or extra parsley for garnish

Instructions:

1. Prep the Mushrooms:
   - Preheat your oven to 375°F (190°C). Clean the mushrooms by wiping them with a damp paper towel or a clean kitchen cloth. Remove the stems and set them aside.

2. Prepare the Filling:
   - In a bowl, combine the Italian-style bread crumbs, grated Parmesan cheese, minced garlic, chopped fresh parsley, and a pinch of salt and black pepper. If you like a bit of heat, you can also add a pinch of red pepper flakes.

3. Make the Mushroom Caps:
   - Take each mushroom cap and lightly brush it with olive oil on the outside. Place them, top-side down, on a baking sheet lined with parchment paper or aluminum foil.

4. Fill the Mushrooms:
   - Take the reserved mushroom stems and finely chop them. Add the chopped stems to the filling mixture and mix well.
   - Fill each mushroom cap generously with the prepared filling, pressing it down slightly to ensure it stays in place.

5. Bake:
   - Place the stuffed mushrooms in the preheated oven and bake for approximately 20-25 minutes, or until the mushrooms are tender and the filling is golden brown.

6. Garnish and Serve:

· Remove the stuffed mushrooms from the oven and let them cool slightly. If desired, garnish with fresh basil leaves or extra chopped parsley.

7. Enjoy:

· Serve your delicious Stuffed Mushrooms as an appetizer or party snack. They're bursting with savory flavors and make for a delightful bite-sized treat. Enjoy!

Mini Spring Rolls Recipe

Ingredients:

For the Spring Rolls:

- 12-15 spring roll wrappers (small-sized)
- 1 cup thinly sliced cabbage
- 1/2 cup thinly sliced carrots
- 1/2 cup thinly sliced bell peppers (any color)
- 1/2 cup bean sprouts (optional)
- 1/2 cup cooked and shredded chicken, shrimp, or tofu (optional)
- 2 tablespoons vegetable oil, for stir-frying
- Salt and pepper, to taste
- Water (for sealing the rolls)
- Vegetable oil, for frying (about 1 cup)

For the Dipping Sauce:

- 1/4 cup soy sauce
- 2 tablespoons rice vinegar
- 1 tablespoon honey or sugar
- 1 clove garlic, minced
- 1/2 teaspoon grated fresh ginger
- 1/2 teaspoon red pepper flakes (adjust to taste, for spiciness)

Instructions:

1. Prepare the Filling:
- In a large skillet or wok, heat 2 tablespoons of vegetable oil over medium-high heat. Add the sliced cabbage, carrots, bell peppers, and bean sprouts (if using). Stir-fry for 2-3 minutes until the vegetables are slightly softened. If you're adding protein (chicken, shrimp, or tofu), stir it in and cook until heated through. Season with salt and pepper to taste. Remove the filling from the heat and let it cool.

2. Assemble the Spring Rolls:

- Take one spring roll wrapper and place it on a clean, dry surface, with one corner pointing toward you (diamond shape).

- Place a spoonful of the cooled filling in the center of the wrapper, leaving some space on each side.

- Fold the bottom corner of the wrapper over the filling, tucking it snugly underneath.

- Fold the left and right corners over the center, creating an envelope shape.

- Moisten the top corner with a little water and roll the wrapper tightly away from you, sealing the roll. The water will help glue the wrapper together.

- Repeat the process with the remaining wrappers and filling.

3. Heat the Oil:

- In a deep skillet or wok, heat about 1 cup of vegetable oil over medium-high heat until it reaches 350-375°F (180-190°C). You can test the oil's readiness by dropping a small piece of wrapper into the oil; if it sizzles and rises to the surface, the oil is hot enough.

4. Fry the Spring Rolls:

- Carefully add 2-3 spring rolls at a time to the hot oil, seam side down. Fry for 2-3 minutes, turning occasionally, until they are golden brown and crispy.

- Using a slotted spoon or tongs, remove the spring rolls from the oil and drain on paper towels to remove excess oil.

5. Prepare the Dipping Sauce:

- In a small bowl, whisk together the soy sauce, rice vinegar, honey or sugar, minced garlic, grated ginger, and red pepper flakes (adjust the spiciness to your liking).

6. Serve:

- Serve the mini spring rolls hot with the dipping sauce on the side. They are best enjoyed immediately while crispy and warm.

7. Enjoy:

- These mini spring rolls make a delightful appetizer or snack, perfect for parties, gatherings, or as a tasty treat any time you're craving a crunchy and flavorful snack.

Thai Egg Rolls with Peanut Sauce Appetizer Recipe

Ingredients

For the Egg Rolls:

- 1 tablespoon vegetable oil
- 2 cloves garlic, minced
- 1 cup shredded cabbage
- 1/2 cup shredded carrots
- 1/2 cup thinly sliced bell peppers
- 1/2 cup bean sprouts
- 1/2 cup cooked, finely chopped chicken or tofu (optional)
- 2 tablespoons soy sauce
- 1 teaspoon sesame oil
- 1 teaspoon sugar
- 1/4 teaspoon ground black pepper
- 10-12 egg roll wrappers
- Vegetable oil, for frying

For the Peanut Sauce:

- 1/2 cup creamy peanut butter
- 2 tablespoons soy sauce
- 1 tablespoon lime juice
- 1 tablespoon honey or brown sugar
- 1 clove garlic, minced
- 1/2 teaspoon grated fresh ginger
- 1/4 teaspoon red pepper flakes (adjust for spiciness)
- Warm water, as needed to thin

Instructions

1. Prepare the Filling:
- Heat 1 tablespoon of vegetable oil in a large skillet over medium heat.

- Add the minced garlic and sauté for 30 seconds.

- Add the shredded cabbage, carrots, bell peppers, and bean sprouts. Stir-fry for 3-4 minutes until the vegetables are tender but still crisp.

- If using, add the chicken or tofu and stir to combine.

- Stir in soy sauce, sesame oil, sugar, and black pepper. Cook for another minute.

- Remove from heat and allow to cool slightly.

2. Assemble the Egg Rolls:

- Place an egg roll wrapper on a clean surface, with one corner pointing towards you.

- Place about 2 tablespoons of the filling near the bottom corner.

- Fold the bottom corner over the filling, roll snugly halfway, fold sides in, then continue rolling. Use a little water to seal the final corner.

- Repeat with the remaining wrappers and filling.

3. Fry the Egg Rolls:

- Heat enough vegetable oil in a deep pan to cover the egg rolls.

- Once hot, fry the egg rolls in batches, turning occasionally, until golden brown and crispy, about 2-3 minutes.

- Remove with a slotted spoon and drain on paper towels.

4. Make the Peanut Sauce:

- In a small bowl, whisk together peanut butter, soy sauce, lime juice, honey or brown sugar, minced garlic, ginger, and red pepper flakes.

- Add warm water a tablespoon at a time until the sauce reaches your desired consistency.

5. Serve:

- Serve the hot egg rolls with the peanut sauce for dipping.

6. Enjoy!

- Enjoy this delicious Thai-inspired appetizer, perfect for gatherings or as a flavorful snack.

BBQ Meatball Appetizer Recipe

Ingredients:

For the Meatballs:

- 1 pound ground beef or a mix of beef and pork
- 1/2 cup breadcrumbs
- 1/4 cup milk
- 1/4 cup finely chopped onion
- 1/4 cup finely chopped green bell pepper (optional)
- 1 egg
- 1/2 teaspoon salt
- 1/4 teaspoon black pepper
- 1/4 teaspoon garlic powder
- 1/4 teaspoon onion powder
- Cooking spray or vegetable oil for greasing

For the BBQ Sauce:

- 1 cup barbecue sauce (your favorite brand or homemade)
- 1/4 cup ketchup
- 2 tablespoons brown sugar
- 1 tablespoon Worcestershire sauce
- 1/2 teaspoon garlic powder
- 1/2 teaspoon onion powder

Instructions:

1. Preheat the Oven:

- Preheat your oven to 375°F (190°C). Line a baking sheet with aluminum foil and lightly grease it with cooking spray or vegetable oil.

2. Prepare the Meatballs:

- In a large mixing bowl, combine the ground beef (or beef/- pork mixture), breadcrumbs, milk, chopped onion, chopped green bell pepper (if using), egg, salt, black pepper, garlic powder, and onion powder. Mix until all the ingredients are well combined.

3. Shape the Meatballs:

-   Using your hands, shape the mixture into small meatballs, approximately 1 inch in diameter. Place the meatballs on the prepared baking sheet, leaving some space between each.

4. Bake the Meatballs:

-   Bake the meatballs in the preheated oven for about 20-25 minutes or until they are cooked through and browned on the outside. The internal temperature of the meatballs should reach 165°F (74°C).

5. Prepare the BBQ Sauce:

-   While the meatballs are baking, make the BBQ sauce. In a saucepan, combine the barbecue sauce, ketchup, brown sugar, Worcestershire sauce, garlic powder, and onion powder. Heat the sauce over low to medium heat, stirring occasionally, until it's heated through and the brown sugar is fully dissolved. Simmer for a few minutes to let the flavors meld. Remove from heat.

6. Glaze the Meatballs:

-   Once the meatballs are cooked, remove them from the oven. Using tongs or a spoon, dip each meatball into the BBQ sauce, coating it generously, and return it to the baking sheet.

7. Broil for Extra Flavor (Optional):

-   If you want a bit of caramelization and extra flavor, you can set your oven to broil and place the sauced meatballs back in the oven for 1-2 minutes until they get slightly charred on top. Watch them closely to prevent burning.

8. Serve:

-   Transfer the BBQ-glazed meatballs to a serving platter or a slow cooker to keep them warm. Garnish with fresh parsley or chopped green onions if desired. Provide toothpicks or small skewers for easy serving.

9. Enjoy:

-   Serve your BBQ meatball appetizers as a delicious and crowd- pleasing snack or party appetizer. They're perfect for game day, potlucks, or any occasion when you want a savory, saucy treat.

Bagel Pizza Snacks Recipe

Prep Time: 10 minutes | Cook Time: 10 minutes | Total Time: 20 minutes

Yield: 6 bagel pizza snacks

Ingredients:

- 3 plain bagels, sliced in half (you'll have 6 halves)
- 1/2 cup pizza sauce (store-bought or homemade)
- 1 1/2 cups shredded mozzarella cheese
- 1/2 cup mini pepperoni slices or your favorite pizza toppings (e.g., diced bell peppers, sliced olives, cooked sausage, or mushrooms)
- 1/2 teaspoon dried oregano
- 1/4 teaspoon garlic powder (optional)
- Fresh basil leaves or parsley for garnish (optional)

Instructions:

1. Preheat the Oven:

- Preheat your oven to 375°F (190°C) and line a baking sheet with parchment paper or a silicone baking mat.

2. Prep the Bagels:

- Slice the plain bagels in half horizontally, creating 6 bagel halves in total.

3. Toast the Bagels:

- Place the bagel halves cut-side up on the prepared baking sheet. Toast them in the preheated oven for about 5 minutes, just until they start to crisp slightly. This will prevent them from getting soggy when you add the toppings.

4. Add Pizza Sauce:

- Remove the toasted bagels from the oven and spread each bagel half with approximately 1 tablespoon of pizza sauce. You can adjust the amount to your preference.

5. Layer with Cheese and Toppings:

- Sprinkle each bagel half with shredded mozzarella cheese. Be generous with the cheese; it will get nice and melty.
- Add your choice of pizza toppings. Mini pepperoni slices work great for bite-sized snacks, but feel free to customize with your favorite ingredients.

6. Season and Bake:

- Sprinkle dried oregano and, if desired, a pinch of garlic powder over the cheese and toppings.

- Place the topped bagel halves back in the oven and bake for approximately 5-7 minutes, or until the cheese is bubbly and lightly golden brown.

7. Garnish and Serve:

- Remove the bagel pizza snacks from the oven and let them cool for a minute or two. If desired, garnish with fresh basil leaves or parsley.

8. Slice and Enjoy:

- Carefully slice each bagel pizza into quarters or smaller pieces if you prefer bite-sized snacks.

- Serve immediately as a delicious and satisfying snack or appetizer.

- These bagel pizza snacks are a quick and easy way to enjoy the flavors of pizza in a fun and convenient format. You can get creative with your toppings and make them just the way you like!

Cheese Quesadilla Recipe

Prep Time: 5 minutes | Cook Time: 10 minutes | Total Time: 15 minutes

Serving Size: 1 quesadilla

Ingredients:

- 2 large flour tortillas
- 1 1/2 cups shredded cheese (such as cheddar, Monterey Jack, or a Mexican cheese blend)
- 1/4 cup diced bell peppers (any color)
- 1/4 cup diced red onion (optional)
- 1/4 cup sliced black olives (optional)
- 1/4 cup chopped fresh cilantro (optional)
- 2 tablespoons vegetable oil or butter
- Salsa, sour cream, or guacamole (for dipping, optional)

Instructions:

1. Prep the Filling:
- In a bowl, combine the shredded cheese, diced bell peppers, diced red onion (if using), sliced black olives (if using), and chopped fresh cilantro (if using). Toss the mixture to distribute the ingredients evenly.

2. Assemble the Quesadilla:
- Lay one tortilla flat on a clean surface. Sprinkle half of the cheese and vegetable mixture evenly over one half of the tortilla.
- Fold the other half of the tortilla over the cheese and press it down gently.

3. Cook the Quesadilla:
- In a large skillet, heat 1 tablespoon of vegetable oil or melt 1 tablespoon of butter over medium heat.
- Place the assembled quesadilla in the skillet and cook for about 2-3 minutes on each side, or until the tortilla is golden brown and the cheese is melted and gooey. You can use a spatula to press it down slightly while cooking.
- If you prefer, you can use a panini press or a quesadilla maker for an even crispier result.

4. Repeat (if making more):
- If you're making more than one quesadilla, repeat the process with the remaining tortillas and filling mixture.

5. Serve:

- Once cooked to your liking, remove the quesadilla(s) from the skillet or quesadilla maker.

- Let them cool for a minute or two, then slice each quesadilla into wedges.

6. Optional Dipping:

- Serve your cheese quesadillas with salsa, sour cream, or guacamole on the side for dipping, if desired.

7. Enjoy:

- Enjoy your delicious and cheesy quesadilla as a quick snack or a simple meal!

Variations:

- Customize your quesadilla by adding other ingredients like cooked chicken, sautéed mushrooms, spinach, or jalapeño slices for extra flavor and texture.

- Experiment with different types of cheese, such as pepper jack, mozzarella, or Swiss.

- Make it a breakfast quesadilla by adding scrambled eggs and diced ham or bacon.

- For a healthier twist, use whole wheat tortillas and add veggies like spinach or roasted bell peppers.

This cheese quesadilla recipe is versatile, quick to prepare, and perfect for a satisfying snack or a fuss-free meal. Feel free to get creative with the ingredients to suit your tastes!

Potato Skins Recipe

Prep Time: 20 minutes | Cook Time: 1 hour | Total Time: 1 hour 20 minutes

Serving Size: 8 potato skins

Ingredients:

- 4 large russet potatoes
- 2 tablespoons olive oil
- Salt and black pepper, to taste
- 1 cup shredded cheddar cheese
- 1/2 cup cooked bacon bits (about 6 slices of cooked bacon)
- 1/4 cup sliced green onions (optional)
- Sour cream, for serving (optional)

Instructions:

1. Preheat the Oven:
- Preheat your oven to 400°F (200°C).
2. Prepare the Potatoes:
- Scrub the russet potatoes thoroughly and pat them dry with a paper towel.
- Using a fork, pierce each potato several times to allow steam to escape while baking.
3. Bake the Potatoes:
- Place the potatoes directly on the oven rack and bake for about 45-60 minutes, or until they are tender when pierced with a fork.
4. Cool and Cut:
- Remove the baked potatoes from the oven and let them cool for a few minutes until they are cool enough to handle.
- Cut each potato in half lengthwise.
5. Scoop Out the Centers:
- Using a spoon, carefully scoop out most of the flesh from each potato half, leaving about 1/4 inch of potato attached to the skin. Reserve the scooped-out potato for another use (such as mashed potatoes).
6. Brush with Olive Oil:
- Place the hollowed-out potato skins on a baking sheet, skin side down.

- Brush the inside and outside of each potato skin with olive oil, and season them with salt and black pepper.

7. Bake Again:

- Return the potato skins to the oven and bake for an addi- tional 10-15 minutes, or until they become crispy and lightly browned.

8. Add Toppings:

- Remove the potato skins from the oven and sprinkle each one with shredded cheddar cheese and bacon bits.

- Place them back in the oven for another 2-3 minutes, or until the cheese is melted and bubbly.

9. Garnish:

- If desired, sprinkle sliced green onions over the potato skins for a pop of color and freshness.

10. Serve:

- Serve your potato skins hot with a side of sour cream for dipping, if you like.

11. Enjoy:

- Enjoy your homemade potato skins as a delicious appetizer or snack!

Variations:

- Experiment with different toppings like chopped jalapeños, diced tomatoes, or even guacamole.

- For a vegetarian version, skip the bacon and add sautéed mushrooms or caramelized onions.

- Make loaded potato skins by adding sour cream, chives, and extra cheese on top.

These crispy potato skins are a crowd-pleasing favorite that's perfect for parties or game day gatherings. You can get creative with the toppings to suit your preferences!

Deviled Eggs Recipe

Prep Time: 15 minutes | Cook Time: 12 minutes (for boiling eggs) | Total Time: 27 minutes

Serving Size: Makes 12 deviled eggs

Ingredients:

- 6 large eggs
- 2 tablespoons mayonnaise
- 1 teaspoon Dijon mustard
- 1 teaspoon white vinegar
- 1/2 teaspoon salt, or to taste
- 1/4 teaspoon black pepper, or to taste
- Paprika or chopped fresh herbs (such as chives or parsley) for garnish (optional)

Instructions:

1. Hard-Boil the Eggs:
- Place the eggs in a saucepan and cover them with cold water. Ensure there's enough water to submerge the eggs by about an inch.
- Place the saucepan over high heat and bring the water to a rolling boil.
- Once the water reaches a boil, turn off the heat, cover the saucepan with a lid, and let the eggs sit in the hot water for 9-12 minutes (depending on your desired yolk consistency).
- After the desired time, carefully drain the hot water and transfer the eggs to a bowl of ice water to cool rapidly. Let them sit for about 5 minutes.

2. Peel the Eggs:
- Gently tap each egg on a hard surface to crack the shell, then roll it between your hands to loosen the shell. Start peeling from the wider end (where the air pocket is), as it's usually easier to remove the shell from there.
- Rinse the peeled eggs under cold water to remove any remaining shell fragments.

3. Cut and Scoop:
- Slice each hard-boiled egg in half lengthwise. Carefully remove the yolks and place them in a separate bowl.

4. Prepare the Filling:
- Mash the egg yolks with a fork until they are crumbly.

- Add the mayonnaise, Dijon mustard, white vinegar, salt, and black pepper to the mashed yolks. Stir well until the mixture is smooth and creamy.

5. Fill the Eggs:

- Using a small spoon or a pastry bag, fill each egg white half with the yolk mixture. You can also use a resealable plastic bag with the corner snipped off as a makeshift piping bag for a neater presentation.

6. Garnish:

- If desired, sprinkle paprika or chopped fresh herbs (such as chives or parsley) over the top of the deviled eggs for added flavor and a decorative touch.

7. Chill and Serve:

- Refrigerate the deviled eggs for at least 30 minutes before serving to allow the flavors to meld.

8. Enjoy:

- Serve your delicious deviled eggs as an appetizer, snack, or side dish for any occasion.

Variations:

- Get creative with your deviled eggs by adding ingredients like crumbled bacon, chopped pickles, grated cheese, or hot sauce to the yolk mixture for different flavors.

- For a smoky twist, add a pinch of smoked paprika to the yolk mixture.

- Make them spicy by incorporating a dash of cayenne pepper or Sriracha sauce.

- Experiment with different garnishes like capers, pimentos, or sliced green olives.

Deviled eggs are a classic and versatile dish that can be cus- tomized to suit your tastes. Enjoy these creamy and savory bites at your next gathering or as a delightful snack!

Classic Pasta Salad Recipe

Prep Time: 15 minutes | Cook Time: 10 minutes | Total Time: 25 minutes

Serving Size: 8 servings

Ingredients:

For the Salad:

- 8 ounces (about 2 cups) uncooked pasta (such as rotini, penne, or bowtie)
- 1 cup cherry tomatoes, halved
- 1 cup cucumber, diced
- 1/2 cup bell pepper (any color), diced
- 1/2 cup red onion, finely chopped
- 1/2 cup black olives, sliced
- 1/2 cup feta cheese, crumbled
- 1/4 cup fresh parsley, chopped

For the Dressing:

- 1/2 cup mayonnaise
- 1/4 cup Greek yogurt (or sour cream)
- 2 tablespoons red wine vinegar
- 1 tablespoon Dijon mustard
- 1 clove garlic, minced
- 1/2 teaspoon salt, or to taste
- 1/4 teaspoon black pepper, or to taste

Instructions:

1. Cook the Pasta:

- Bring a large pot of salted water to a boil. Add the pasta and cook according to the package instructions until al dente. Drain and rinse the pasta under cold water to cool it down.

2. Prepare the Dressing:

- In a small bowl, whisk together the mayonnaise, Greek yogurt (or sour cream), red wine vinegar, Dijon mustard, minced garlic, salt, and black pepper. Adjust the seasoning to taste.

3. Combine the Ingredients:

· In a large mixing bowl, combine the cooked and cooled pasta, halved cherry tomatoes, diced cucumber, diced bell pepper, finely chopped red onion, sliced black olives, crumbled feta cheese, and chopped fresh parsley.

4. Add the Dressing:

· Pour the prepared dressing over the pasta and vegetables.

5. Toss and Chill:

· Gently toss all the ingredients together until they are well coated with the dressing.

· Cover the bowl and refrigerate the pasta salad for at least 30 minutes to allow the flavors to meld.

6. Serve:

· Before serving, give the pasta salad a quick toss to redistribute the dressing and flavors.

7. Enjoy:

· Serve your classic pasta salad as a side dish or a light summer meal.

Variations:

· Customize your pasta salad by adding other ingredients like diced grilled chicken, ham, or salami for extra protein.

· Incorporate different vegetables such as broccoli florets, baby spinach, or roasted red peppers.

· Experiment with alternative cheeses like mozzarella, ched- dar, or Parmesan.

· For a Mediterranean twist, add chopped Kalamata olives, artichoke hearts, and sun-dried tomatoes.

This classic pasta salad is a crowd-pleasing dish that's perfect for picnics, barbecues, potlucks, or as a refreshing side dish year-round. Feel free to adapt it to your tastes and get creative with the ingredients!

Loaded Nachos Recipe

Prep Time: 10 minutes | Cook Time: 10 minutes | Total Time: 20 minutes

Serving Size: 4 servings

Ingredients:

- 1 bag (about 10-12 ounces) tortilla chips
- 2 cups shredded cheddar cheese (or your favorite cheese blend)
- 1 cup cooked and seasoned ground beef (or use ground turkey or vegetarian meat substitute)
- 1 cup cooked black beans, drained and rinsed
- 1/2 cup sliced jalapeños (adjust to your spice preference)
- 1/2 cup diced tomatoes
- 1/4 cup sliced black olives
- 1/4 cup diced red onion
- 1/4 cup chopped fresh cilantro
- 1/2 cup sour cream
- 1/4 cup salsa
- Guacamole (optional, for serving)
- Sliced green onions (optional, for garnish)
- Pickled jalapeño slices (optional, for garnish)

Instructions:

1. Preheat the Oven:
- Preheat your oven to 350°F (175°C).
2. Layer the Chips:
- Spread a layer of tortilla chips evenly on a large oven-safe serving platter or baking sheet.
3. Add the Toppings:
- Sprinkle half of the shredded cheddar cheese evenly over the chips.
- Layer on the seasoned ground beef, black beans, jalapeños, diced tomatoes, sliced black olives, and diced red onion.
- Top with the remaining shredded cheddar cheese.

4. Bake:

· Place the loaded nachos in the preheated oven and bake for about 10 minutes, or until the cheese is melted and bubbly.

5. Garnish and Serve:

· Remove the nachos from the oven and sprinkle chopped fresh cilantro over the top.

· Serve the loaded nachos hot with sides of sour cream, salsa, and guacamole, if desired.

· Garnish with sliced green onions and pickled jalapeño slices for extra flavor and presentation.

6. Enjoy:

· Dive into your loaded nachos and savor the delicious combi- nation of cheesy, savory, and spicy flavors!

Variations:

· Customize your loaded nachos with additional toppings like sautéed onions and bell peppers, diced avocado, or even shredded lettuce.

· For a vegetarian version, skip the ground meat and use meatless crumbles or roasted vegetables as a replacement.

· Adjust the level of spiciness by adding more or fewer jalapeños or using a milder salsa.

· Make it extra indulgent by drizzling nacho cheese sauce over the top.

Loaded nachos are perfect for sharing with friends and family on game days, movie nights, or as a fun appetizer for parties. Feel free to get creative with your toppings and enjoy the ultimate comfort food!

7 Layer Dip Recipe

This classic 7 Layer Dip is a favorite for parties and gatherings, offering a delightful mix of flavors and textures in each scoop. It's easy to prepare and can be made ahead of time.

Ingredients:

- Refried Beans Layer:
- 1 (16 oz) can of refried beans
- 1 tsp of taco seasoning

Guacamole Layer:

- 3 medium ripe avocados
- 1 lime, juiced
- Salt, to taste
- 2 tbsp of chopped cilantro

Sour Cream Layer:

- 1 cup sour cream
- 1 tsp taco seasoning

Salsa Layer:

- 1 cup of your favorite salsa

Cheese Layer:

- 1 cup shredded cheddar or Mexican blend cheese

Olives Layer:

- ½ cup black olives, sliced

Green Onion Layer:

- ½ cup green onions, chopped

Additional Toppings (optional):

- Chopped tomatoes
- Chopped cilantro
- Sliced jalapeños

Instructions:

1. Prepare the Refried Beans: Mix the refried beans with 1 tsp of taco seasoning. Spread this mixture as the first layer in the bottom of a 9x13 inch dish or a large serving platter.

2. Make the Guacamole: Mash the avocados in a bowl. Mix in lime juice, salt, and chopped cilantro. Spread the guacamole over the bean layer.

3. Sour Cream Layer: Combine the sour cream with 1 tsp of taco seasoning. Spread this over the guacamole layer.

4. Add the Salsa: Carefully spread the salsa over the sour cream layer. If your salsa is very liquidy, you might want to drain it a bit before adding.

5. Cheese Layer: Sprinkle the shredded cheese evenly over the salsa.

6. Add Olives and Green Onions: Scatter the sliced olives and then the chopped green onions over the cheese.

7. Chill and Serve: Refrigerate the dip for at least an hour before serving to allow the flavors to meld. Serve with tortilla chips.

Tips:

- You can customize the layers to your taste. Feel free to add a layer of chopped lettuce, corn, or a different type of bean.
- For a spicier dip, add a layer of chopped jalapeños or use spicy refried beans.
- To keep the guacamole from browning, make sure it's covered with the sour cream layer and store the dip in the fridge until it's time to serve.

Enjoy your delicious and colorful 7 Layer Dip, a perfect appetizer for any gathering!

Homemade Ranch Dip Recipe

Prep Time: 10 minutes | Total Time: 10 minutes

Serving Size: Makes about 1 cup

Ingredients:

- 1/2 cup mayonnaise
- 1/2 cup sour cream
- 1-2 tablespoons fresh chives, finely chopped
- 1-2 tablespoons fresh parsley, finely chopped
- 1 clove garlic, minced
- 1/2 teaspoon dried dill weed (or 1 teaspoon fresh dill, chopped)
- 1/2 teaspoon onion powder
- 1/4 teaspoon salt, or to taste
- 1/4 teaspoon black pepper, or to taste
- 1/2 teaspoon lemon juice (optional)
- 1-2 tablespoons milk (for thinning, optional)

Instructions:

1. Combine the Ingredients:
- In a mixing bowl, whisk together the mayonnaise and sour cream until smooth.

2. Add the Herbs and Spices:
- Stir in the fresh chives, fresh parsley, minced garlic, dried dill weed (or fresh dill), onion powder, salt, and black pepper.

3. Adjust the Consistency (Optional):
- If you prefer a thinner dip, you can add 1-2 tablespoons of milk to achieve your desired consistency.

4. Season with Lemon Juice (Optional):
- If you like a touch of tanginess, you can add 1/2 teaspoon of lemon juice to brighten up the flavors. Adjust to taste.

5. Chill and Serve:
- Cover the bowl and refrigerate the ranch dip for at least 30 minutes to allow the flavors to meld together.

6. Enjoy:

- Serve your homemade ranch dip with fresh vegetable sticks, potato chips, pretzels, or as a flavorful dip for various appetizers.

Variations:

- For a spicy kick, add a pinch of cayenne pepper or a dash of hot sauce.

- Experiment with different herbs like tarragon or cilantro for unique flavors.

- If you prefer a stronger garlic flavor, you can add an extra clove of minced garlic.

- Customize the seasoning by adjusting the salt and black pepper to your taste.

- Make a buttermilk ranch dip by substituting some of the sour cream or mayonnaise with buttermilk.

Homemade ranch dip is a versatile and delicious condiment that pairs well with a wide variety of snacks and appetizers. You can adjust the ingredients to suit your preferences and enjoy the fresh, creamy flavors

French Onion Dip Recipe

Prep Time: 10 minutes | Cook Time: 30 minutes (caramelizing onions) | Total Time: 40 minutes

Serving Size: Makes about 2 cups

Ingredients:

- 2 large yellow onions, thinly sliced
- 2 tablespoons unsalted butter
- 1 tablespoon olive oil
- 1 teaspoon sugar
- 1 teaspoon salt
- 1/2 teaspoon black pepper
- 1 cup sour cream
- 1/2 cup mayonnaise
- 1 teaspoon Worcestershire sauce
- 1/2 teaspoon garlic powder
- 1/2 teaspoon onion powder
- Fresh chives or parsley, for garnish (optional)
- Potato chips, pretzels, or fresh vegetables for dipping

Instructions:

1. Caramelize the Onions:

- In a large skillet, melt the butter and olive oil over medium- low heat. Add the thinly sliced onions and cook, stirring occasionally, for about 20-30 minutes until they become golden brown and caramelized.

- During the last few minutes of cooking, sprinkle the sugar, salt, and black pepper over the onions. Stir to combine and continue cooking until they reach a deep caramel color.

2. Let the Onions Cool:

- Remove the caramelized onions from the skillet and let them cool to room temperature.

3. Prepare the Dip:

- In a mixing bowl, combine the sour cream, mayonnaise, Worcestershire sauce, garlic powder, and onion powder.

- Once the caramelized onions have cooled, add them to the mixture. Stir well to evenly distribute the onions throughout the dip.

4. Chill and Serve:

- Cover the bowl and refrigerate the French onion dip for at least 30 minutes to allow the flavors to meld together.

- Before serving, garnish with fresh chives or parsley if desired.

5. Serve:

- Serve your homemade French Onion Dip with potato chips, pretzels, or fresh vegetable sticks for dipping.

6. Enjoy:

- Enjoy the rich and savory flavors of this classic dip!

Variations:

- For a lighter version, you can use low-fat sour cream and light mayonnaise.

- Add a touch of grated Parmesan cheese for extra richness.

- Experiment with different herbs and spices, like thyme or smoked paprika, to customize the flavor.

- If you prefer a creamier consistency, blend the caramelized onions with the sour cream and mayonnaise mixture using a food processor or blender.

This homemade French Onion Dip is perfect for parties, gather- ings, or simply enjoying as a snack. The caramelized onions bring a sweet and savory depth of flavor to this classic dip, making it a crowd-pleaser.

Homemade Guacamole Recipe

Prep Time: 10 minutes | Total Time: 10 minutes

Serving Size: Makes about 2 cups

Ingredients:

- 3 ripe avocados
- 1 medium tomato, diced
- 1/2 cup finely diced red onion
- 1/4 cup chopped fresh cilantro
- 2 cloves garlic, minced
- 1-2 jalapeño peppers, seeded and minced (adjust to your preferred level of spiciness)
- Juice of 1 lime
- Salt and black pepper, to taste

Instructions:

1. Prepare the Avocados:

- Cut the avocados in half lengthwise. Remove the pits and scoop the flesh into a mixing bowl.

2. Mash the Avocado:

- Use a fork or potato masher to mash the avocado to your desired level of smoothness. Some people prefer it slightly chunky, while others like it smoother.

3. Add the Ingredients:

- Add the diced tomato, finely diced red onion, chopped cilantro, minced garlic, and minced jalapeño peppers to the mashed avocado.
- Squeeze the juice of one lime over the mixture. This not only adds flavor but also helps prevent the avocados from browning.

4. Season and Mix:

- Season the guacamole with salt and black pepper to taste.
- Gently mix all the ingredients together until well combined.

5. Taste and Adjust:

- Taste the guacamole and adjust the seasoning if needed. You can add more salt, lime juice, or minced jalapeño if desired.

6. Serve:

· Transfer the guacamole to a serving bowl.

7. Garnish (optional):

· If you like, you can garnish the guacamole with additional chopped cilantro or a few slices of jalapeño for presentation.

8. Enjoy:

· Serve your homemade guacamole with tortilla chips, fresh vegetable sticks, or as a topping for tacos, burritos, or nachos.

Variations:

· Customize your guacamole by adding diced red bell pepper, corn kernels, or black beans for extra flavor and texture.

· For a creamy twist, mix in a dollop of sour cream or Greek yogurt.

· Experiment with different spices like cumin or chili powder to enhance the flavor.

· If you prefer a smoother guacamole, use a food processor or blender for a finer texture.

This homemade guacamole is a versatile and delicious dip or topping that's perfect for parties, snacks, or adding a burst of flavor to your favorite Mexican dishes. Enjoy the creamy, fresh, and zesty goodness of homemade guacamole!

Homemade Salsa Recipe

Prep Time: 10 minutes | Total Time: 10 minutes

Serving Size: Makes about 2 cups

Ingredients:

- 4 ripe tomatoes, diced
- 1/2 cup finely chopped red onion
- 1/4 cup chopped fresh cilantro
- 2 cloves garlic, minced
- 1-2 jalapeño peppers, seeded and minced (adjust to your preferred level of spiciness)
- Juice of 1 lime
- 1 teaspoon ground cumin
- Salt and black pepper, to taste

Instructions:

1. Dice the Tomatoes:
- Cut the tomatoes into small dice. You can remove the seeds and excess liquid if you prefer a thicker salsa.
2. Prepare the Vegetables:
- Finely chop the red onion, fresh cilantro, and jalapeño peppers. Mince the garlic cloves.
3. Combine the Ingredients:
- In a mixing bowl, combine the diced tomatoes, chopped red onion, chopped cilantro, minced garlic, and minced jalapeño peppers.
4. Season the Salsa:
- Squeeze the juice of one lime over the mixture.
- Add the ground cumin, salt, and black pepper to taste.
5. Mix Well:
- Gently stir all the ingredients together until well combined.
6. Taste and Adjust:
- Taste the salsa and adjust the seasoning if needed. You can add more salt, lime juice, or minced jalapeño if you want it spicier.
7. Serve:
- Transfer the homemade salsa to a serving bowl.

8. Enjoy:

- Serve your fresh homemade salsa with tortilla chips, tacos, grilled meats, or as a topping for nachos or burritos.

Variations:

- Customize your salsa by adding diced bell peppers, corn kernels, or black beans for extra flavor and texture.
- If you prefer a smoky flavor, consider adding a pinch of smoked paprika.
- For a milder salsa, remove the seeds and membranes from the jalapeño peppers.
- Experiment with different types of chili peppers for varying levels of heat and flavor.
- If you like your salsa to have a hint of sweetness, add a teaspoon of honey or agave nectar.

This homemade salsa is a versatile and flavorful condiment that adds a fresh and zesty kick to your favorite Mexican and Tex- Mex dishes. Enjoy the vibrant flavors of this classic salsa!

Sundried Tomato Spread

Prep Time: 10 minutes | Total Time: 10 minutes

Servings: Approximately 1 1/2 cups of spread

Ingredients:

- 1/2 cup sundried tomatoes (dry or oil-packed), drained if necessary
- 1/2 cup crumbled feta cheese
- 1/4 cup pitted black olives
- 2 cloves garlic, minced
- 1/4 cup extra-virgin olive oil
- Salt and black pepper, to taste
- Bagel chips or Triscuits (for serving)

Instructions:

1. Prepare the Ingredients:
- If you're using dry sundried tomatoes, soak them in hot water for about 10-15 minutes to rehydrate them. Drain and pat dry.
2. Combine the Ingredients:
- In a food processor, add the rehydrated or oil-packed sun- dried tomatoes, crumbled feta cheese, pitted black olives, and minced garlic.
- Pulse the mixture several times until the ingredients are finely chopped and well combined.
3. Drizzle with Olive Oil:
- With the food processor running, slowly drizzle in the extra-virgin olive oil until the spread reaches your desired consistency. You may need a little more or less olive oil depending on your preference.
4. Season to Taste:
- Taste the spread and season with salt and black pepper as needed. Keep in mind that both feta cheese and olives can be salty, so be cautious with the salt.
5. Serve:
- Transfer the sundried tomato and feta spread to a serving bowl.
6. Enjoy:
- Serve your homemade sundried tomato and feta spread with bagel chips or Triscuits. It's a flavorful and savory spread that's perfect for snacking, appetizers, or as a topping for your favorite dishes.
- This sundried tomato and feta spread combines the rich flavors of sundried tomatoes, tangy feta cheese, and briny black olives, making it a delicious accompaniment to your favorite crackers or chips or spreads for wraps and sandwiches. Enjoy the Mediterranean-inspired goodness!

Basic Hummus Recipe

Ingredients:

- 1 can (15 ounces) chickpeas (garbanzo beans), drained and rinsed
- 1/4 cup fresh lemon juice (about 1 large lemon)
- 1/4 cup tahini (sesame paste)
- 1 small garlic clove, minced (adjust to taste)
- 2 tablespoons extra-virgin olive oil, plus more for serving
- 1/2 teaspoon ground cumin
- Salt, to taste
- 2 to 3 tablespoons ice water
- Optional garnishes: Paprika, chopped fresh parsley, addi- tional olive oil, or pine nuts

Instructions:

1. Prepare the Chickpeas:
- Drain and rinse the chickpeas in a colander under cold running water. Removing the skins from the chickpeas is optional but can result in smoother hummus.
2. Combine Ingredients:
- In a food processor, combine the chickpeas, lemon juice, tahini, minced garlic, olive oil, ground cumin, and a pinch of salt.
3. Blend Until Smooth:
- Process the mixture until it's well blended and reaches a smooth and creamy consistency. You may need to stop and scrape down the sides of the food processor bowl with a spatula to ensure all the ingredients are fully incorporated.
4. Adjust the Texture:
- If the hummus appears too thick, add 2 to 3 tablespoons of ice water, one tablespoon at a time, while the food processor is running. Continue processing until the hummus reaches your desired texture. Adding ice water helps make the hummus creamier.
5. Taste and Adjust:
- Taste the hummus and adjust the seasoning. You can add more salt, lemon juice, or minced garlic according to your preference. Blend again to incorporate any additional ingredients.
6. Serve:
- Transfer the hummus to a serving dish. If desired, create a well in the center with the back of a spoon and drizzle extra olive oil into the well. This is a traditional garnish.

7. Garnish (Optional):

· Sprinkle paprika, chopped fresh parsley, or toasted pine nuts on top for added flavor and presentation.

8. Enjoy:

· Serve your homemade basic hummus with pita bread, fresh vegetables, or as a dip for your favorite snacks. It's also a versatile spread for sandwiches and wraps.

Note: Homemade hummus can be stored in an airtight container in the refrigerator for up to one week. Before serving leftovers, you may need to stir the hummus and drizzle a little olive oil on top to refresh its consistency and flavor.

Dinner Mains

Chicken Breast Recipe

Prep Time: 10 minutes | Cook Time: 15-18 minutes | Total Time: 25-28 minutes

Servings: 2

Ingredients:

- 2 boneless, skinless chicken breasts
- 2 tablespoons olive oil
- 2 cloves garlic, minced
- 1 teaspoon paprika
- 1/2 teaspoon dried oregano
- 1/2 teaspoon dried thyme
- Salt and black pepper, to taste
- 1 lemon, sliced for garnish (optional)
- Fresh parsley, chopped, for garnish (optional)

Instructions:

1. Preheat the Skillet:
- Place a large skillet (preferably cast iron) on the stovetop over medium-high heat. Add the olive oil and let it heat up.
2. Season the Chicken:
- While the skillet is heating, season the chicken breasts on both sides with paprika, dried oregano, dried thyme, salt, and black pepper.
3. Sear the Chicken:
- Once the skillet is hot, carefully add the seasoned chicken breasts to the pan. Sear them for about 6-8 minutes on the first side, or until they develop a golden brown crust.
4. Flip and Continue Cooking:
- Flip the chicken breasts over and cook for another 6-8 min- utes on the second side, or until the internal temperature reaches 165°F (74°C) and the chicken is no longer pink in the center. The total cooking time may vary depending on the thickness of the chicken breasts.
5. Add Garlic:
- In the last 2 minutes of cooking, add the minced garlic to the skillet. Sauté it with the chicken until fragrant, being careful not to burn the garlic.

6. Rest and Serve:

- Remove the skillet-grilled chicken breasts from the heat and let them rest for a couple of minutes. This allows the juices to redistribute, ensuring a juicy result.

7. Garnish and Serve:

- Garnish the chicken with lemon slices and fresh chopped parsley if desired.

8. Serve:

- Serve your skillet-grilled chicken breast hot as a delicious main course. It pairs well with a variety of side dishes like roasted vegetables, rice, or a fresh salad.

Enjoy your perfectly cooked, flavorful chicken breasts made in a skillet — a quick and convenient way to enjoy grilled chicken indoors!

Chicken, Rice, and Broccoli Casserole Recipe

Ingredients

- 2 cups cooked rice (white or brown)
- 2 cups cooked, shredded chicken (rotisserie chicken works well)
- 1 medium head of broccoli, cut into florets
- 1 cup sour cream
- 1 can (10.5 oz) cream of chicken soup
- 1 cup shredded cheddar cheese
- 1/2 cup milk
- 1 small onion, finely chopped
- 2 cloves garlic, minced
- 1/2 teaspoon paprika
- Salt and pepper, to taste
- Optional: 1/2 cup bread crumbs or crushed crackers for topping
- Optional: 2 tablespoons melted butter (if using bread crumbs or crackers)

Instructions

1. Preheat the Oven:
- Preheat your oven to 350°F (175°C). Grease a 9x13 inch baking dish.
2. Prepare the Broccoli:
- Steam the broccoli florets until just tender, about 3-4 minutes. You want them to retain some bite as they will continue to cook in the oven.
3. Combine the Ingredients:
- In a large bowl, mix together the cooked rice, shredded chicken, and steamed broccoli.
- Add the sour cream, cream of chicken soup, half of the cheddar cheese, milk, onion, garlic, paprika, salt, and pepper. Stir well to combine.
4. Assemble the Casserole:
- Spread the mixture evenly into the prepared baking dish.
- Sprinkle the remaining cheddar cheese over the top.
- If using, mix the bread crumbs or crushed crackers with melted butter and sprinkle over the casserole.

5. Bake the Casserole:

· Bake uncovered in the preheated oven for 30-35 minutes, or until the casserole is bubbly and the top is golden brown.

6. Serve and Enjoy:

· Allow the casserole to sit for a few minutes before serving.

· Serve hot as a comforting and hearty meal.

This Chicken, Rice, and Broccoli Casserole is a classic comfort food dish that's both easy to make and satisfying. It's perfect for a simple family dinner, with its creamy texture and a delightful blend of flavors that everyone can enjoy.

Crispy Fried Chicken Recipe

Prep Time: 30 minutes (plus 2-4 hours for marinating) | Cook Time: 20-25 minutes | Total Time: 50-55 minutes

Servings: 4-6

Ingredients:

For the Marinade:

- 2-3 pounds chicken pieces (drumsticks, thighs, wings, or breast)
- 1 cup buttermilk
- 1 teaspoon salt
- 1/2 teaspoon black pepper
- 1/2 teaspoon paprika
- 1/2 teaspoon garlic powder
- 1/2 teaspoon onion powder
- 1/4 teaspoon cayenne pepper (adjust to your desired level of heat)

For the Coating:

- 2 cups all-purpose flour
- 1 tablespoon paprika
- 1 tablespoon garlic powder
- 1 tablespoon onion powder
- 1 tablespoon dried thyme
- 1 tablespoon dried oregano
- 1 teaspoon salt
- 1 teaspoon black pepper
- Vegetable oil, for frying

Instructions:

1. Marinate the Chicken:

- In a large bowl, combine the buttermilk, salt, black pepper, paprika, garlic powder, onion powder, and cayenne pepper to create the marinade.
- Place the chicken pieces in the marinade, ensuring they are well-coated. Cover the bowl and refrigerate for at least 2-4 hours, or preferably overnight. This step helps tenderize the chicken and infuses it with flavor.

2. Prepare the Coating Mixture:

- In a shallow dish, combine the all-purpose flour, paprika, garlic powder, onion powder, dried thyme, dried oregano, salt, and black pepper. Mix well to create the coating mixture.

3. Coat the Chicken:

· Remove the marinated chicken pieces from the refrigerator and allow them to come to room temperature for about 30 minutes.

· Heat vegetable oil in a large skillet or Dutch oven to a depth of about 2 inches over medium-high heat. Use a thermometer to ensure the oil reaches 350-375°F (175-190°C).

· Take each chicken piece, allowing excess marinade to drip off, and coat it thoroughly with the flour mixture. Press the coating onto the chicken to ensure it adheres well.

4. Fry the Chicken:

· Carefully place the coated chicken pieces in the hot oil, making sure not to overcrowd the pan. Fry in batches if necessary.

· Fry the chicken for about 10-15 minutes per side, or until it reaches an internal temperature of 165°F (74°C) and the coating is deep golden brown and crispy.

5. Drain and Rest:

· Use a slotted spoon or tongs to remove the fried chicken from the hot oil. Place them on a wire rack or a plate lined with paper towels to drain any excess oil. Allow the chicken to rest for a few minutes.

This homemade fried chicken recipe yields wonderfully crispy and flavorful chicken with a tender and juicy interior. It's a classic comfort food that's perfect for family dinners and gatherings. We recommend serving with Roasted Potatoes and Cole Slaw.

Chicken Stir-Fry Recipe

Prep Time: 15 minutes | Cook Time: 10 minutes | Total Time: 25 minutes

Servings: 4

Ingredients:

For the Marinade:

- 1 pound boneless, skinless chicken breasts or thighs, cut into bite-sized pieces
- 2 tablespoons soy sauce
- 1 tablespoon rice vinegar
- 1 teaspoon cornstarch
- 1/2 teaspoon sugar
- 1/4 teaspoon black pepper

For the Stir-Fry Sauce:

- 1/4 cup low-sodium soy sauce
- 2 tablespoons oyster sauce (optional)
- 1 tablespoon hoisin sauce
- 1 tablespoon rice vinegar
- 1 teaspoon sesame oil
- 1 teaspoon cornstarch
- 1/2 teaspoon sugar

For the Stir-Fry:

- 2 tablespoons vegetable oil, divided
- 2 cloves garlic, minced
- 1-inch piece of fresh ginger, minced
- 1 red bell pepper, sliced
- 1 yellow bell pepper, sliced
- 1 cup broccoli florets
- 1 cup snap peas, trimmed
- 1 carrot, sliced thinly
- 1 cup sliced mushrooms
- 1/2 cup baby corn (optional)
- 1/4 cup water or chicken broth

- 2 green onions, chopped, for garnish
- Sesame seeds, for garnish (optional)

Instructions:

1. Marinate the Chicken:

- In a bowl, combine the soy sauce, rice vinegar, cornstarch, sugar, and black pepper to create the marinade.
- Add the chicken pieces to the marinade, ensuring they are well-coated. Let it marinate for at least 10 minutes while you prepare the other ingredients.

2. Prepare the Stir-Fry Sauce:

- In a separate bowl, whisk together the soy sauce, oyster sauce (if using), hoisin sauce, rice vinegar, sesame oil, cornstarch, and sugar to create the stir-fry sauce. Set it aside.

3. Heat the Pan:

- Heat 1 tablespoon of vegetable oil in a large skillet or wok over high heat.

4. Stir-Fry the Chicken:

- Remove the chicken from the marinade, allowing any excess liquid to drain off. Add the chicken to the hot skillet and stir- fry for 2-3 minutes or until it's no longer pink. Remove the chicken from the skillet and set it aside.

5. Stir-Fry the Vegetables:

- In the same skillet, add the remaining 1 tablespoon of vegetable oil. Add the minced garlic and ginger, and stir-fry for about 30 seconds until fragrant.
- Add the sliced bell peppers, broccoli, snap peas, carrot, mushrooms, and baby corn (if using). Stir-fry for 3-4 minutes or until the vegetables are tender-crisp.

6. Combine Chicken and Vegetables:

- Return the cooked chicken to the skillet with the vegetables.

7. Add Stir-Fry Sauce:

- Pour the prepared stir-fry sauce over the chicken and vegetables.
- Add the water or chicken broth to the skillet to create more sauce. Stir everything together.
- Cook and Garnish:
- Cook for an additional 2-3 minutes, or until the sauce has thickened and coats the chicken and vegetables.
- Garnish the chicken stir-fry with chopped green onions and sesame seeds, if desired.

8. Serve:

- Serve your chicken stir-fry hot over cooked rice or noodles for a delicious and satisfying meal.

This chicken stir-fry is a quick and flavorful way to enjoy a variety of vegetables and tender, marinated chicken in a savory sauce. It's a perfect weeknight dinner option that's both healthy and delicious.

Chicken Enchiladas Recipe

Prep Time: 20 minutes | Cook Time: 30 minutes | Total Time: 50 minutes

Servings: 4-6

Ingredients:

For the Chicken Filling:

- 2 cups shredded cooked chicken (rotisserie chicken works well)
- 1 small onion, finely chopped
- 1 bell pepper, finely chopped
- 2 cloves garlic, minced
- 1 cup canned black beans, drained and rinsed
- 1 cup corn kernels (fresh, frozen, or canned)
- 1 teaspoon ground cumin
- 1/2 teaspoon chili powder
- Salt and black pepper, to taste
- 1 cup shredded Monterey Jack or cheddar cheese

For the Enchilada Sauce:

- 2 cups red enchilada sauce (store-bought or homemade)
- 1/2 cup sour cream
- 1/2 cup chopped fresh cilantro (optional)
- Salt and black pepper, to taste

For Assembling and Baking:

- 10-12 small corn or flour tortillas
- 1 cup shredded cheese (Monterey Jack or cheddar) for top- ping
- Sliced green onions and chopped fresh cilantro for garnish (optional)

Instructions:

1. Preheat the Oven:
- Preheat your oven to 350°F (175°C).

2. Prepare the Chicken Filling:

- In a large skillet, heat a little oil over medium heat. Add the chopped onion and bell pepper. Sauté for about 3-4 minutes until they start to soften.

- Add the minced garlic and sauté for another 30 seconds until fragrant.

- Stir in the shredded chicken, black beans, corn, ground cumin, chili powder, salt, and black pepper. Cook for 2-3 minutes until everything is heated through and well combined. Remove from heat.

3. Make the Enchilada Sauce:

- In a mixing bowl, combine the red enchilada sauce and sour cream. Mix until well blended. If you like it spicier, you can add some hot sauce or extra chili powder to taste. Season with salt and black pepper as needed. Stir in the chopped cilantro if desired.

4. Assemble the Enchiladas:

- Warm the tortillas briefly in the microwave or on a griddle to make them more pliable.

- Spoon a small amount of the chicken mixture into each tortilla, roll it up tightly, and place it seam-side down in a greased 9x13-inch baking dish.

- Continue filling and rolling until all the tortillas are used.

5. Pour the Enchilada Sauce:

- Pour the enchilada sauce mixture evenly over the rolled tortillas in the baking dish.

6. Add Cheese and Bake:

- Sprinkle the shredded cheese over the top of the enchiladas.

- Cover the baking dish with aluminum foil and bake in the preheated oven for 20-25 minutes, or until the enchiladas are heated through, and the cheese is melted and bubbly.

7. Garnish and Serve:

- Remove the foil and bake for an additional 5-10 minutes, or until the cheese is golden brown and slightly crispy.

- Garnish with sliced green onions and chopped cilantro, if desired.

8. Serve:

- Serve your chicken enchiladas hot with a side of Mexican rice, guacamole, and sour cream.

Enjoy your homemade chicken enchiladas with their rich, creamy sauce and flavorful filling — a perfect dish for a family dinner or a casual get-together!

Chicken Parmesan Recipe

Prep Time: 20 minutes | Cook Time: 25 minutes | Total Time: 45 minutes

Servings: 4

Ingredients:

For the Chicken:

- 4 boneless, skinless chicken breasts
- Salt and black pepper, to taste
- 1 cup all-purpose flour, for dredging
- 2 large eggs
- 2 cups Italian-style breadcrumbs
- 1 cup grated Parmesan cheese
- 1/4 cup fresh parsley, chopped
- 2 cups marinara sauce (homemade or store-bought)
- 1 1/2 cups shredded mozzarella cheese
- 1/4 cup olive oil, for frying
- Fresh basil leaves, for garnish (optional)

For the Pasta (Optional):

- 8 ounces spaghetti or your favorite pasta
- Olive oil
- Salt and black pepper
- Grated Parmesan cheese, for serving

Instructions:

1. Preheat the Oven:
- Preheat your oven to 400°F (200°C).
2. Prepare the Chicken:
- Season the chicken breasts with salt and black pepper to taste.
3. Dredge the Chicken:
- Dredge each chicken breast in the all-purpose flour, shaking off any excess.
4. Egg Wash:
- In a shallow dish, whisk the eggs.
5. Bread the Chicken:
- In another shallow dish, combine the Italian-style breadcrumbs, grated Parmesan cheese, and chopped fresh pars- ley.

- Dip each chicken breast into the whisked eggs, allowing any excess to drip off, and then coat it evenly with the breadcrumb mixture. Press the breadcrumbs onto the chicken to ensure they adhere well.

6. Fry the Chicken:

- In a large ovenproof skillet, heat the olive oil over medium- high heat. Once hot, add the breaded chicken breasts and cook for about 2-3 minutes on each side, or until they are golden brown and crispy.

7. Add Marinara Sauce:

- Spoon marinara sauce over the top of each chicken breast.

8. Add Cheese:

- Sprinkle shredded mozzarella cheese over the sauce.

9. Bake:

- Transfer the skillet to the preheated oven and bake for about 15-20 minutes, or until the chicken is cooked through, the cheese is melted and bubbly, and the sauce is hot and bubbly.

10. Serve:

- Serve the chicken Parmesan hot, garnished with fresh basil leaves if desired.

11. Enjoy:

- Enjoy your homemade chicken Parmesan with pasta or as a delicious standalone dish. We recommend Fettuccine Alfredo. We have provided a recipe in "on the side" Chapter.

This chicken Parmesan recipe is a comforting classic that com- bines crispy breaded chicken with savory marinara sauce and gooey melted cheese. It's perfect for a family dinner or a special occasion meal.

Chicken, Corn, and Salsa Skillet Meal

Prep Time: 10 minutes | Cooking Time: 20 minutes | Total Time: 30 minutes

Servings: 4

Ingredients:

- 1 pound boneless, skinless chicken breasts, cubed
- 2 tablespoons olive oil
- 1 onion, finely chopped
- 1 bell pepper, diced (any color)
- 1 can (15 ounces) corn kernels, drained (or 1 1/2 cups frozen corn, thawed)
- 1 cup salsa (mild, medium, or hot, depending on your preference)
- 1 teaspoon ground cumin
- 1 teaspoon chili powder
- Salt and black pepper, to taste
- 4 large tortillas or cooked rice (for serving)
- Optional toppings: shredded cheese, sour cream, chopped cilantro, lime wedges

Instructions:

1. Cook the Chicken:

- Heat the olive oil in a large skillet over medium-high heat.
- Add the cubed chicken to the skillet, season with salt, black pepper, ground cumin, and chili powder.
- Cook the chicken, stirring occasionally, until it's browned and cooked through, about 5-7 minutes. Remove the cooked chicken from the skillet and set it aside.

2. Sauté the Vegetables:

- In the same skillet, add the chopped onion and diced bell pepper. Sauté for 3-4 minutes, or until the vegetables become tender.

3. Add Corn and Salsa:

- Stir in the drained corn kernels and salsa into the skillet with the sautéed vegetables. Mix well.

4. Combine and Simmer:

- Return the cooked chicken to the skillet with the vegetable mixture. Stir everything together.
- Reduce the heat to low and let the mixture simmer for about 5-7 minutes, allowing the flavors to meld.

5. Serve:

· Serve the chicken, corn, and salsa mixture in warm tortillas as tacos or burritos. Alternatively, you can serve it over cooked rice.

6. Add Toppings (Optional):

· Customize your meal by adding your favorite toppings like shredded cheese, sour cream, chopped cilantro, or a squeeze of lime juice.

7. Enjoy:

· Enjoy your delicious and easy-to-make chicken, corn, and salsa skillet meal. It's a versatile dish that's perfect for a quick weeknight dinner.

This flavorful skillet meal combines tender chicken with sweet corn, savory salsa, and aromatic spices for a satisfying and vibrant dish. It's a great option for a fuss-free dinner or a delightful filling for tortillas or rice bowls.

Skillet-Cooked Steak Recipe

Prep Time: 5 minutes | Cook Time: 10-15 minutes | Total Time: 15-20 minutes

Servings: 2

Ingredients:

- 2 boneless ribeye, sirloin, or New York strip steaks (about 1 inch thick)
- 2 tablespoons olive oil or vegetable oil
- 2 cloves garlic, minced (optional)
- Salt and black pepper, to taste
- 2 tablespoons butter (optional)
- Fresh herbs (rosemary, thyme, or parsley) for garnish (optional)

Equipment:

- Cast-iron skillet or heavy-bottomed skillet
- Tongs

Instructions:

1. Prepare the Steaks:

- Remove the steaks from the refrigerator and let them sit at room temperature for 30 minutes. This allows them to cook more evenly.
- Pat the steaks dry with paper towels to remove any excess moisture, which helps with searing.

2. Preheat the Skillet:

- Place your cast-iron skillet or heavy-bottomed skillet on the stovetop over medium-high heat. Let it get very hot. You'll know it's ready when you can hold your hand 1 inch above the skillet and feel the heat.

3. Season the Steaks:

- Brush both sides of the steaks with olive oil and season generously with salt and black pepper. Add minced garlic if desired.

4. Sear the Steaks:

- Carefully place the seasoned steaks in the hot skillet using tongs. Be cautious, as the skillet and oil will be very hot.
- Sear the steaks for 3-5 minutes on each side for medium- rare, depending on the thickness of the steak and your desired level of doneness. Adjust the cooking time for your preferred doneness: 2-3 minutes for rare, 5-7 minutes for medium, and 8-10 minutes for well-done.

5. Add Butter (Optional):

·   If desired, during the last 1-2 minutes of cooking, add butter to the skillet and let it melt. Baste the steaks with the melted butter by tilting the skillet and spooning the butter over the top of the steaks. This adds extra flavor and richness.

6. Rest the Steaks:

·   Remove the steaks from the skillet and transfer them to a plate. Allow them to rest for about 5 minutes. This allows the juices to redistribute, resulting in a more tender and juicy steak.

7. Slice and Garnish:

·   Slice the steaks against the grain into thin strips. Garnish with fresh herbs, such as rosemary, thyme, or parsley, if desired.

8. Serve:

·   Serve your skillet-cooked steaks immediately with your favorite side dishes, like mashed potatoes, sautéed vegetables, or a salad.

Enjoy your perfectly seared and flavorful skillet-cooked steaks! Adjust the cooking time to your preferred level of doneness for the best steak experience.

Beef Stew in the Slow Cooker Recipe

Ingredients

- 2 pounds beef stew meat, cut into 1-inch pieces
- 1/4 cup all-purpose flour
- 1/2 teaspoon salt
- 1/2 teaspoon black pepper
- 2 tablespoons olive oil
- 1 medium onion, chopped
- 2 cloves garlic, minced
- 3 cups beef broth
- 1/2 cup red wine (optional)
- 2 tablespoons tomato paste
- 1 teaspoon dried thyme
- 1 teaspoon dried rosemary
- 2 bay leaves
- 3 large carrots, peeled and sliced
- 3 medium potatoes, peeled and cubed
- 1 cup frozen peas
- Salt and pepper, to taste
- Optional: Chopped fresh parsley for garnish

Instructions

1. Prep the Beef:
- In a large bowl, toss the beef stew meat with flour, salt, and pepper until well coated.
2. Brown the Beef:
- Heat olive oil in a skillet over medium-high heat. Add the beef in batches and sear on all sides until browned. Transfer the browned beef to the slow cooker.
3. Sauté the Aromatics:
- In the same skillet, add the chopped onion and cook until translucent. Add the minced garlic and cook for an additional minute. Transfer to the slow cooker.
4. Deglaze the Pan (optional):

- Pour the red wine into the skillet and scrape up any browned bits from the bottom of the pan. Add this liquid to the slow cooker.

- Add Remaining Ingredients:

- To the slow cooker, add the beef broth, tomato paste, thyme, rosemary, and bay leaves. Stir to combine.

- Add the sliced carrots and cubed potatoes to the mixture.

5. Cook the Stew:

- Cover and cook on low for 7-8 hours or on high for 3-4 hours, until the beef is tender.

6. Finish the Stew:

- About 30 minutes before serving, stir in the frozen peas.

- Adjust seasoning with additional salt and pepper to taste.

- Remove the bay leaves.

7. Serve:

- Ladle the beef stew into bowls.

- Garnish with chopped fresh parsley if desired.

8. Enjoy!

- Enjoy this hearty and comforting beef stew, perfect for a cold day or a cozy night in.

This slow cooker beef stew is the epitome of comfort food, with tender chunks of beef, flavorful vegetables, and a rich, hearty broth. It's an ideal recipe for busy days, as the slow cooker does most of the work for you.

Slow Cooker Pot Roast Recipe

Prep Time: 15 minutes | Cooking Time: 6-8 hours on low heat |Total Time: 6 hours 15 minutes to 8 hours 15 minutes

Servings: 6

Ingredients:

- 3-4 pounds chuck roast
- 2 tablespoons vegetable oil
- 2 onions, sliced
- 4 cloves garlic, minced
- 4 carrots, peeled and cut into chunks
- 4 potatoes, peeled and cut into chunks
- 2 celery stalks, chopped
- 1 cup beef broth
- 1/2 cup red wine (optional)
- 2 bay leaves
- 2 sprigs fresh thyme (or 1 teaspoon dried thyme)
- 2 sprigs fresh rosemary (or 1 teaspoon dried rosemary)
- Salt and black pepper, to taste
- 2 tablespoons cornstarch (optional, for thickening)

Instructions:

1. Sear the Roast:
- Season the chuck roast generously with salt and black pepper.
- Heat the vegetable oil in a large skillet or on the stovetop in your slow cooker insert (if it's safe for stovetop use).
- Sear the roast on all sides until it's browned. This step adds flavor to the meat. Remove the roast from the skillet or slow cooker insert and set it aside.
2. Prep the Vegetables:
- In the same skillet or slow cooker insert, add the sliced onions and minced garlic. Sauté for a few minutes until they become fragrant.
3. Assemble in the Slow Cooker:
- Place the seared roast in the slow cooker.

- Add the sautéed onions and garlic on top of the roast.

- Arrange the carrots, potatoes, and celery around the roast.

- Pour in the beef broth and red wine (if using).

- Add the bay leaves, thyme, and rosemary sprigs.

4. Cook the Pot Roast:

- Cover the slow cooker and cook on low heat for 6-8 hours or until the roast is tender and can be easily shredded with a fork.

5. Optional Thickening (Gravy):

- About 30 minutes before serving, you can thicken the cook- ing liquid to make a gravy. To do this, mix 2 tablespoons of cornstarch with 2 tablespoons of cold water to create a slurry. Stir the slurry into the cooking liquid and let it cook for a few more minutes until thickened.

6. Serve:

- Remove the bay leaves, thyme sprigs, and rosemary sprigs.

- Slice or shred the pot roast and serve it with the vegetables and gravy.

7. Enjoy:

- Serve your slow cooker pot roast with a side of warm crusty bread, mashed potatoes, or your favorite vegetables. This comforting meal is perfect for a hearty dinner with your loved ones.

Sloppy Joes Recipe

Prep Time: 10 minutes | Cooking Time: 20 minutes | Total Time: 30 minutes

Servings: 4-6

Ingredients:

- 1 pound ground beef (or ground turkey for a leaner option)
- 1 medium onion, finely chopped
- 1 green bell pepper, finely chopped
- 2 cloves garlic, minced
- 1/2 cup ketchup
- 1/4 cup tomato sauce
- 2 tablespoons brown sugar
- 1 tablespoon Worcestershire sauce
- 1 teaspoon yellow mustard
- 1/2 teaspoon chili powder (adjust to taste)
- Salt and black pepper, to taste
- Hamburger buns, for serving

Instructions:

1. Brown the Ground Meat:

- In a large skillet or frying pan over medium-high heat, add the ground beef. Break it apart with a spatula and cook until it's browned and no longer pink. Drain any excess fat if necessary.

2. Sauté the Vegetables:

- Add the finely chopped onion and green bell pepper to the skillet with the cooked ground beef. Sauté for about 3-4 minutes, or until the vegetables become tender.

3. Add the Garlic and Seasonings:

- Stir in the minced garlic and cook for an additional 1-2 minutes until fragrant.
- Add the brown sugar, Worcestershire sauce, yellow mustard, and chili powder to the skillet. Stir to combine.

4. Combine with Tomato Sauce:

- Pour in the ketchup and tomato sauce, and season with salt and black pepper to taste. Mix well.

5. Simmer the Mixture:

- Reduce the heat to low, cover the skillet, and let the mixture simmer for about 10-15 minutes, stirring occasionally. This allows the flavors to meld and the sauce to thicken.

6. Taste and Adjust:

- Taste the sloppy joe mixture and adjust the seasoning, adding more salt, pepper, or chili powder if needed to suit your taste.

7. Serve:

- Spoon the hot sloppy joe mixture onto hamburger buns.

8. Enjoy:

- Serve immediately, and enjoy your homemade sloppy joes with a side of coleslaw, pickles, or potato chips.

Sloppy Joes are a classic American comfort food, perfect for a quick and satisfying meal. You can customize them by adding your favorite toppings like cheese, sliced pickles, or jalapeños.

Simple Meatloaf Recipe

Prep Time: 15 minutes | Cook Time: 1 hour | Total Time: 1 hour 15 minutes

Servings: 6

Ingredients:

- · For the Meatloaf:
- · 2 pounds ground beef (80% lean)
- · 1 envelope (1 ounce) Lipton Onion Soup Mix
- · 1/2 cup ketchup
- · 1/2 cup breadcrumbs
- · 1 large egg
- · Salt and black pepper, to taste

For the Glaze:

- · 1/4 cup ketchup
- · 2 tablespoons brown sugar
- · 1 teaspoon Dijon mustard (optional)

Instructions:

1. Preheat the Oven:
- · Preheat your oven to 350°F (175°C).
2. Combine the Meatloaf Ingredients:
- · In a large mixing bowl, combine the ground beef, Lipton Onion Soup Mix, 1/2 cup of ketchup, breadcrumbs, and the large egg. Season with salt and black pepper to taste.
3. Mix Well:
- · Use your hands or a spatula to thoroughly mix the ingredi- ents until everything is well combined. Avoid overmixing, as it can make the meatloaf dense.
4. Shape the Meatloaf:
- · Transfer the meatloaf mixture to a greased or parchment- lined 9x5-inch loaf pan. Shape it into a loaf shape, pressing down slightly to even it out.
5. Make the Glaze:
- · In a small bowl, mix together the 1/4 cup of ketchup, brown sugar, and Dijon mustard (if using) to create the glaze.

6. Glaze the Meatloaf:

· Spread the glaze evenly over the top of the meatloaf.

7. Bake:

· Place the meatloaf in the preheated oven and bake for approximately 1 hour, or until the internal temperature reaches 160°F (71°C) and the top is nicely browned.

8. Rest and Serve:

· Remove the meatloaf from the oven and let it rest for about 10 minutes before slicing. This allows the juices to redistribute and makes for easier slicing.

9. Slice and Enjoy:

· Slice the meatloaf into portions and serve it hot.

This straightforward meatloaf recipe uses the classic com- bination of ground beef, Lipton Onion Soup Mix, ketchup, breadcrumbs, and egg to create a tasty and comforting meal that's sure to please your taste buds. Recommend serving with Mashed Potatoes and Steamed Peas.

Homemade Spaghetti and Meatballs

Prep Time: 30 minutes | Cook Time: 1 hour 30 minutes | Total Time: 2 hours

Servings: 4-6

Ingredients:

For the Sauce:

- 2 tablespoons olive oil
- 1 onion, finely chopped
- 2 carrots, peeled and grated
- 4 cloves garlic, minced
- 1 (28-ounce) can crushed tomatoes
- 1 (14-ounce) can diced tomatoes
- 2 teaspoons dried basil
- 1 teaspoon dried oregano
- Salt and black pepper, to taste
- Pinch of red pepper flakes (optional, for heat)
- 1 teaspoon sugar (optional, to balance acidity)

For the Meatballs:

- 1 pound ground beef (or a mix of beef and pork)
- 1/2 cup breadcrumbs
- 1/4 cup grated Parmesan cheese
- 1/4 cup milk
- 1/4 cup fresh parsley, finely chopped
- 1/4 cup onion, finely chopped
- 2 cloves garlic, minced
- 1 egg
- Salt and black pepper, to taste
- Olive oil (for frying)

For Serving:

- 12 ounces spaghetti
- Fresh basil leaves, chopped (for garnish)
- Grated Parmesan cheese (for serving)

Instructions:

For the Sauce:

1. Sauté the Aromatics:

- In a large saucepan, heat the olive oil over medium heat. Add the finely chopped onion, grated carrots, and minced garlic. Sauté for about 5 minutes until the vegetables soften.

2. Add Tomatoes and Seasonings:

- Stir in the crushed tomatoes, diced tomatoes (with their juices), dried basil, dried oregano, salt, black pepper, and a pinch of red pepper flakes if you want some heat. Option- ally, add a teaspoon of sugar to balance the acidity of the tomatoes.

3. Simmer:

- Bring the sauce to a gentle simmer, then reduce the heat to low. Cover and let it simmer for at least 30 minutes, stirring occasionally. The longer it simmers, the more flavorful it will become.

For the Meatballs:

1. Prepare the Meatball Mixture:

- In a large mixing bowl, combine the ground beef, bread- crumbs, grated Parmesan cheese, milk, finely chopped fresh parsley, finely chopped onion, minced garlic, egg, salt, and black pepper. Mix until all ingredients are well combined.

2. Form the Meatballs:

- Using your hands, shape the mixture into golf ball-sized meatballs (about 2 inches in diameter). You should get approximately 12 meatballs.

3. Fry the Meatballs:

- In a large skillet, heat olive oil over medium-high heat. Add the meatballs and cook, turning occasionally, until they are browned on all sides and cooked through, about 10-15 minutes. Ensure they are cooked to an internal temperature of 160°F (71°C).

4. Add the Meatballs to the Sauce:

- Once the meatballs are cooked, gently transfer them to the simmering carrot-based sauce. Let them simmer together for an additional 15-20 minutes to allow the flavors to meld.

For Serving:

1. Cook the Spaghetti:

- While the meatballs are simmering in the sauce, cook the spaghetti according to the package instructions until al dente. Drain and set aside.

2. Plate the Dish:

- Serve the spaghetti topped with the carrot-based sauce and meatballs. Garnish with chopped fresh basil and grated Parmesan cheese.

3. Enjoy:

- Enjoy your homemade spaghetti and meatballs with a fla- vorful, veggie-infused sauce!

This hearty and satisfying spaghetti and meatballs recipe com- bines the classic comfort of meatballs with a rich and tasty carrot-based tomato sauce. It's a family favorite that's perfect for a comforting dinner. Recom- mend serving with Caesar Salad and Garlic Bread!

No-Boil Spinach Lasagna Recipe

Prep Time: 20 minutes | Cook Time: 40-45 minutes | Total Time: 60-65 minutes

Servings: 8

Ingredients:

- 9 lasagna noodles (no-boil or oven-ready)
- 1 pound ground beef or Italian sausage (optional)
- 1 medium onion, finely chopped
- 3 cloves garlic, minced
- 1 (24-ounce) jar of marinara sauce
- 1 (15-ounce) container ricotta cheese
- 1 egg
- 2 cups shredded mozzarella cheese
- 1 cup grated Parmesan cheese
- 1 (10-ounce) package frozen chopped spinach, thawed and squeezed dry
- 1 teaspoon dried basil
- 1 teaspoon dried oregano
- Salt and black pepper, to taste
- Fresh basil or parsley, for garnish (optional)

Instructions:

1. Preheat the Oven:
- Preheat your oven to 375°F (190°C).
2. Brown the Meat (Optional):
- In a large skillet over medium-high heat, cook the ground beef or Italian sausage until it's no longer pink. Break it apart into crumbles as it cooks. If you're using sausage links, remove the casings first.
- Remove any excess fat from the pan.
3. Add Onion and Garlic:
- Add the finely chopped onion and minced garlic to the skillet. Sauté for 2-3 minutes until the onion is translucent and the garlic is fragrant. If you're not using meat, simply sauté the onion and garlic in a bit of olive oil until softened.
4. Combine with Marinara Sauce:
- Pour the marinara sauce into the skillet with the meat, onion, and garlic. Stir well to combine. Simmer for a few minutes to heat through. Season with salt, black pepper, dried basil, and dried oregano to

taste.

5. Prepare the Cheese Mixture:

- In a mixing bowl, combine the ricotta cheese, egg, shredded mozzarella, grated Parmesan, thawed and drained chopped spinach, dried basil, dried oregano, salt, and black pepper. Mix until well combined.

6. Assemble the Lasagna:

- In a 9x13-inch baking dish, spread a thin layer of the meat sauce to prevent sticking.

- Place three uncooked lasagna noodles on top of the sauce.

- Spread a third of the cheese mixture evenly over the noodles.

- Repeat the layers until all ingredients are used, finishing with a layer of sauce on top. Make sure to reserve some mozzarella and Parmesan cheese for topping.

7. Bake:

- Cover the baking dish with aluminum foil and bake in the preheated oven for 30-35 minutes.

8. Add Cheese Topping:

- Remove the foil and sprinkle the remaining mozzarella and Parmesan cheese over the lasagna.

9. Continue Baking:

- Return the uncovered lasagna to the oven and bake for an additional 10-15 minutes, or until the cheese is bubbly and golden brown.

10. Rest and Serve:

- Allow the lasagna to rest for a few minutes before slicing.

11. Garnish and Enjoy:

- Optionally, garnish with fresh basil or parsley before serving.

12. Serve:

- Serve your delicious no-boil spinach lasagna with a side salad and garlic bread for a satisfying meal.

This no-boil spinach lasagna is a convenient and flavorful twist on the classic dish. It's perfect for a family dinner or for feeding a crowd, and the no-boil noodles make it a time-saving option.

Taco Recipe with Seasoned Ground Beef

Prep Time: 10 minutes | Cook Time: 15 minutes | Total Time: 25 minutes

Servings: 4-6

Ingredients:

- · For the Seasoned Ground Beef:
- · 1 pound lean ground beef
- · 1 packet taco seasoning mix (or 2 tablespoons homemade taco seasoning)
- · 1/4 cup water

For Assembling Tacos:

- · 8-12 small taco shells or tortillas (hard or soft, your choice)
- · 1 cup shredded lettuce
- · 1 cup diced tomatoes
- · 1 cup shredded cheddar or Mexican blend cheese
- · 1/2 cup diced onions
- · 1/2 cup sliced black olives (optional)
- · Sour cream, salsa, and guacamole for garnish (optional)
- · Jalapeño slices for extra heat (optional)

Instructions:

1. Brown the Ground Beef:
- · In a large skillet over medium-high heat, cook the lean ground beef, breaking it apart with a spatula as it cooks. Cook until it's no longer pink, about 5-7 minutes.
2. Season the Beef:
- · Once the beef is browned, drain any excess fat from the skillet.
- · Sprinkle the taco seasoning mix over the cooked beef. Add 1/4 cup of water and stir well to combine. Simmer for 2-3 minutes, or until the mixture thickens and the beef is fully coated in seasoning.
3. Warm the Taco Shells:
- · While the beef is simmering, warm your taco shells or tortillas according to the package instructions. You can use soft tortillas, hard taco shells, or your preferred taco vessel.

4. Assemble the Tacos:

- Place a spoonful of the seasoned ground beef into each taco shell or tortilla.

- Top with shredded lettuce, diced tomatoes, diced onions, black olives (if using), and shredded cheese.

5. Garnish and Serve:

- Add a dollop of sour cream, a spoonful of salsa, and a scoop of guacamole if desired.

- For those who like it spicy, garnish with jalapeño slices.

6. Serve Hot:

- Serve your delicious homemade tacos immediately, and enjoy!

This taco recipe with seasoned ground beef is a crowd-pleasing favorite that you can customize with your favorite toppings and sauces. It's a quick and easy meal that's perfect for a weeknight dinner or a fun family taco night.

Breaded Pork Chops Recipe

Prep Time: 15 minutes | Cook Time: 20 minutes | Total Time: 35 minutes

Servings: 4 pork chops

Ingredients:

- For the Pork Chops:
- 4 boneless pork chops (about 1 inch thick)
- Salt and black pepper, to taste
- 1 cup all-purpose flour
- 2 large eggs
- 2 tablespoons milk
- 1 1/2 cups breadcrumbs (preferably Panko breadcrumbs for extra crispiness)
- 1/2 cup grated Parmesan cheese (optional)
- 1 teaspoon dried thyme (optional)
- 1/2 teaspoon garlic powder (optional)
- 1/2 teaspoon paprika (optional)
- Cooking oil (vegetable, canola, or peanut oil) for frying

For the Optional Lemon-Garlic Butter Sauce:

- 2 tablespoons unsalted butter
- 2 cloves garlic, minced
- Juice of 1/2 lemon
- Fresh parsley, chopped (for garnish)

Instructions:

1. Preheat the Oven:
- Preheat your oven to 200°F (93°C). This will keep the cooked pork chops warm while you prepare the rest of the meal.
2. Prepare the Pork Chops:
- Pat the pork chops dry with paper towels. Season them on both sides with salt and black pepper.
3. Set Up Breading Station:
- In three separate shallow bowls, set up a breading station.

- Place the flour in the first bowl, whisk the eggs with milk in the second bowl, and combine the breadcrumbs (and optional Parmesan cheese, dried thyme, garlic powder, and paprika) in the third bowl.

4. Bread the Pork Chops:

- Dredge each pork chop in the flour, making sure it's coated evenly. Shake off any excess.

- Dip the floured pork chops into the egg mixture, ensuring they are well coated.

- Finally, press each pork chop into the breadcrumb mixture, firmly coating both sides. You can gently press the bread- crumbs onto the pork chops to help them adhere.

5. Heat the Oil:

- In a large skillet, heat about 1/4 inch of cooking oil over medium-high heat until it reaches 350-375°F (180-190°C). You can test the oil's readiness by dropping a breadcrumb into it; if it sizzles and turns golden brown, the oil is ready.

6. Fry the Pork Chops:

- Carefully place the breaded pork chops into the hot oil. Cook for approximately 3-4 minutes per side, or until they are golden brown and the internal temperature reaches 145°F (63°C) for medium doneness. Adjust the cooking time if you prefer your pork chops more or less cooked.

7. Drain and Keep Warm:

- Remove the fried pork chops from the skillet and place them on a wire rack or a paper towel-lined plate to drain any excess oil. Keep them warm in the preheated oven while you prepare any optional sauce.

Optional Lemon-Garlic Butter Sauce:

1. Make the Sauce:

- In a small saucepan, melt the butter over medium heat. Add the minced garlic and cook for about 1 minute until fragrant but not browned.

- Remove the saucepan from heat and stir in the lemon juice.

2. Serve:

- Drizzle the lemon-garlic butter sauce over the breaded pork chops.

3. Garnish and Enjoy:

4. Garnish the pork chops with fresh chopped parsley.

Serve your crispy and flavorful breaded pork chops hot, accom- panied by your favorite side dishes. We recommend Macaroni and Cheese and steamed Green Beans. Enjoy your delicious homemade meal!

Pork Tenderloin with Dijon Mustard Sauce Recipe

Prep Time: 10 minutes | Cook Time: 25-30 minutes | Total Time: 35-40 minutes

Servings: 4

Ingredients:

- For the Pork Tenderloin:
- 2 pork tenderloins (about 1 to 1.5 pounds each)
- 2 tablespoons olive oil
- 2 cloves garlic, minced
- 1 teaspoon dried thyme
- 1 teaspoon dried rosemary
- Salt and black pepper, to taste

For the Dijon Mustard Sauce:

- 1/2 cup heavy cream
- 3 tablespoons Dijon mustard
- 2 tablespoons whole-grain mustard
- 2 tablespoons butter
- Salt and black pepper, to taste
- Fresh parsley, chopped, for garnish (optional)

Instructions:

1. Preheat the Oven:
- Preheat your oven to 375°F (190°C).
2. Season the Pork Tenderloin:
- In a small bowl, mix together the minced garlic, dried thyme, dried rosemary, salt, and black pepper.
- Rub the pork tenderloins all over with this herb and garlic mixture.
3. Sear the Pork:
- In an ovenproof skillet or pan, heat the olive oil over medium-high heat. Once hot, add the pork tenderloins and sear them for 2-3 minutes per side until they are nicely browned.

4. Roast in the Oven:

- Transfer the skillet to the preheated oven and roast the pork for 15-20 minutes or until the internal temperature reaches 145°F (63°C) for medium-rare to 160°F (71°C) for medium. The exact cooking time may vary based on the thickness of your pork tenderloins.

5. Rest the Pork:

- Remove the pork from the oven and place it on a cutting board. Cover it loosely with aluminum foil and let it rest for about 5-10 minutes. This allows the juices to redistribute, ensuring a juicy and tender result.

6. Prepare the Dijon Mustard Sauce:

- While the pork is resting, prepare the Dijon mustard sauce. In a saucepan over medium heat, combine the heavy cream, Dijon mustard, whole-grain mustard, and butter.

- Stir continuously until the sauce is heated through and the butter has melted. Season with salt and black pepper to taste. Allow the sauce to simmer for a few minutes until it thickens slightly.

7. Slice and Serve:

- Slice the rested pork tenderloins into medallions.

- Serve the sliced pork drizzled with the creamy Dijon mustard sauce.

8. Garnish and Enjoy:

- Optionally, garnish with chopped fresh parsley for a burst of color and freshness.

9. Serve Hot:

- Serve your pork tenderloin with Dijon mustard sauce im- mediately for a flavorful and elegant meal. We recommend baked potato and vegetables.

This pork tenderloin with Dijon mustard sauce is a delicious and impressive dish that's perfect for a special dinner at home. The creamy sauce complements the tender and well-seasoned pork beautifully.

Pulled Pork Recipe

Prep Time: 15 minutes | Cook Time: 6-8 hours (slow cooker) or 4-6 hours (oven) | Total Time: 6-8 hours (slow cooker) or 4-6 hours (oven)

Servings: 8-10

Ingredients:

For the Pork:

- 4-5 pounds boneless pork shoulder (also known as pork butt)
- 2 tablespoons vegetable oil
- 1 large onion, sliced
- 4 cloves garlic, minced
- 1 cup chicken or vegetable broth
- 2 bay leaves
- 1 teaspoon dried thyme
- 1 teaspoon paprika
- 1/2 teaspoon cayenne pepper (adjust to your spice prefer- ence)
- Salt and black pepper, to taste

For the BBQ Sauce (optional):

- 1 1/2 cups BBQ sauce of your choice

For Serving:

- Hamburger buns or soft rolls
- Coleslaw (optional)

Instructions:

1. Preheat the Oven (if not using a slow cooker):

- If you're not using a slow cooker, preheat your oven to 300°F (150°C).

2. Sear the Pork (Optional):

- In a large skillet or ovenproof pot, heat the vegetable oil over medium-high heat. If you have a slow cooker with a searing function, you can do this directly in the slow cooker.

- Season the pork shoulder with salt and black pepper. Sear the pork on all sides until it's browned, about 3-5 minutes per side. This step is optional but adds extra flavor.

3. Prepare the Slow Cooker or Pot:

    · If using a slow cooker, transfer the seared pork shoulder to the slow cooker. If using an ovenproof pot, keep the pork in the pot.

4. Add Aromatics and Liquid:

    · Scatter the sliced onion, minced garlic, bay leaves, dried thyme, paprika, and cayenne pepper around the pork.

    · Pour in the chicken or vegetable broth. The liquid should come about halfway up the side of the pork.

5. Slow Cooker Method:

    · If using a slow cooker, cover it and cook on LOW for 6-8 hours or until the pork is very tender and falls apart easily with a fork.

6. Oven Method:

    · If using an ovenproof pot, cover it with a tight-fitting lid or heavy-duty foil. Place it in the preheated oven and cook for 4-6 hours, or until the pork is tender and shreds easily.

7. Shred the Pork:

    · Once the pork is done, remove it from the slow cooker or pot and transfer it to a large cutting board or a large bowl.

    · Use two forks to shred the pork into bite-sized pieces. Discard any excess fat and the bay leaves.

8. Optional BBQ Sauce:

    · If you like your pulled pork saucy, you can mix in your favorite BBQ sauce with the shredded pork. Start with 1 cup and add more to your taste.

9. Serve:

    · Serve the pulled pork on hamburger buns or soft rolls.

    · You can also top it with coleslaw for a classic Southern-style pulled pork sandwich.

10. Enjoy:

    · Enjoy your homemade pulled pork sandwiches with your choice of side dishes or on their own.

This pulled pork recipe results in tender, flavorful pulled pork that's perfect for sandwiches, sliders, or serving with your favorite sides. It's a great option for feeding a crowd or enjoying leftovers for several meals.

Fish Tacos Recipe

Prep Time: 20 minutes | Cook Time: 10 minutes | Total Time: 30 minutes

Servings: 4

Ingredients:

For the Fish:

- 1 pound white fish fillets (such as cod, tilapia, or mahi- mahi)
- 1/2 cup all-purpose flour
- 1 teaspoon chili powder
- 1/2 teaspoon paprika
- Salt and black pepper, to taste
- 1 cup buttermilk
- 1 cup panko breadcrumbs
- Vegetable oil for frying

For the Cabbage Slaw:

- 2 cups shredded green cabbage
- 1/4 cup mayonnaise
- 2 tablespoons lime juice
- 1 teaspoon honey or sugar
- Salt and black pepper, to taste

For Assembling the Tacos:

- 8 small flour or corn tortillas
- Sliced avocado
- Sliced red onion
- Fresh cilantro leaves
- Lime wedges
- Hot sauce or salsa (optional)

Instructions:

1. Prepare the Fish:

- Cut the fish fillets into strips or manageable-sized pieces.

- In a shallow dish, combine the flour, chili powder, paprika, salt, and black pepper.

- Dip each piece of fish into the buttermilk, allowing any excess to drip off.

- Coat the fish in the seasoned flour mixture, pressing the coating onto the fish to adhere.

- Dip the coated fish back into the buttermilk and then into the panko breadcrumbs, pressing the breadcrumbs onto the fish to form an even coating.

2. Fry the Fish:

- Heat vegetable oil in a large skillet or frying pan over medium-high heat until it reaches 350°F (175°C).

- Carefully add the breaded fish pieces to the hot oil and fry for about 2-3 minutes per side, or until the fish is golden brown and cooked through. Drain on paper towels.

3. Make the Cabbage Slaw:

- In a bowl, combine the shredded green cabbage, mayon- naise, lime juice, honey or sugar, salt, and black pepper. Toss to coat the cabbage evenly. Adjust seasoning to taste.

4. Warm the Tortillas:

- Heat the tortillas in a dry skillet over medium heat or in the microwave for a few seconds until warm and pliable.

5. Assemble the Tacos:

- Place a generous spoonful of the cabbage slaw on each tortilla.

- Top with the fried fish, sliced avocado, sliced red onion, and fresh cilantro leaves.

6. Serve and Garnish:

- Serve the fish tacos with lime wedges and hot sauce or salsa on the side for those who like it spicy.

7. Enjoy:

- Enjoy your homemade fish tacos as a delicious and satisfy- ing meal.

Fish tacos are a flavorful and refreshing dish with a delightful combination of crispy fish, creamy slaw, and fresh toppings. They make a great choice for a casual dinner or a summer cookout.

Shrimp Scampi Recipe

Ingredients:

- 1 pound large shrimp, peeled and deveined
- 8 ounces linguine or spaghetti
- 4 tablespoons unsalted butter
- 2 tablespoons olive oil
- 4 cloves garlic, minced
- 1/4 teaspoon red pepper flakes (adjust to taste, for spiciness)
- 1/2 cup dry white wine
- Juice of 1 lemon
- 2 tablespoons fresh parsley, chopped
- Salt and black pepper, to taste
- Grated Parmesan cheese, for garnish (optional)
- Lemon wedges, for serving (optional)

Instructions:

1. Cook the Pasta:

- Bring a large pot of salted water to a boil. Add the linguine or spaghetti and cook according to the package instructions until al dente. Drain and set aside.

2. Sauté the Shrimp:

- In a large skillet, heat the olive oil and 2 tablespoons of butter over medium-high heat. Add the minced garlic and red pepper flakes and sauté for about 30 seconds until fragrant.

- Add the peeled and deveined shrimp to the skillet. Cook for 1-2 minutes per side, or until they turn pink and opaque. Remove the cooked shrimp from the skillet and set them aside.

3. Make the Scampi Sauce:

- In the same skillet, add the dry white wine and lemon juice. Bring the mixture to a simmer and let it cook for about 2 minutes, allowing the alcohol to evaporate and the sauce to reduce slightly.

- Stir in the remaining 2 tablespoons of butter and chopped fresh parsley. Season with salt and black pepper to taste. Stir until the sauce thickens and the butter melts.

4. Combine with Pasta:

- Return the cooked shrimp to the skillet, along with any accumulated juices. Toss the shrimp in the scampi sauce to heat them through.

- Add the cooked linguine or spaghetti to the skillet. Toss everything together to coat the pasta and shrimp evenly with the sauce.

5. Garnish and Serve:

- Serve the Shrimp Scampi hot, garnished with grated Parme- san cheese and lemon wedges if desired.

6. Enjoy:

- Enjoy your delicious Shrimp Scampi over linguine or with crusty bread for dipping. This dish is bursting with the flavors of garlic, lemon, white wine, and succulent shrimp, making it a delightful Italian-inspired seafood treat.

Shrimp Linguini Recipe

Ingredients:

- 8 ounces linguini pasta
- 1 pound large shrimp, peeled and deveined
- 2 tablespoons olive oil
- 4 cloves garlic, minced
- 1/2 teaspoon red pepper flakes (adjust to taste, for spiciness)
- 1 cup cherry tomatoes, halved
- 1/2 cup dry white wine (optional)
- 1/2 cup chicken or vegetable broth
- 1/4 cup heavy cream
- Zest and juice of 1 lemon
- 1/4 cup fresh basil leaves, chopped
- Salt and black pepper, to taste
- Grated Parmesan cheese, for garnish (optional)

Instructions:

1. Cook the Linguini:

- Bring a large pot of salted water to a boil. Add the linguini pasta and cook according to the package instructions until al dente. Drain and set aside.

2. Season and Cook the Shrimp:

- Season the shrimp with a pinch of salt and black pepper. In a large skillet, heat the olive oil over medium-high heat. Add the minced garlic and red pepper flakes, and sauté for about 30 seconds until fragrant.

- Add the seasoned shrimp to the skillet and cook for 1- 2 minutes per side, or until they turn pink and opaque. Remove the cooked shrimp from the skillet and set them aside.

3. Make the Sauce:

- In the same skillet, add the halved cherry tomatoes and cook for 2-3 minutes until they begin to soften.

- If using, pour in the white wine to deglaze the pan, scraping up any browned bits from the bottom. Allow the wine to simmer for a couple of minutes until it reduces by half.

- Stir in the chicken or vegetable broth, heavy cream, lemon zest, and lemon juice. Simmer for another 2-3 minutes to combine the flavors and thicken the sauce slightly.

4. Combine and Toss:

·   Return the cooked shrimp to the skillet, along with any accumulated juices. Add the chopped fresh basil and toss everything together to heat the shrimp and combine the ingredients.

5. Add the Linguini:

·   Gently fold the cooked linguini into the skillet with the shrimp and sauce. Toss to coat the pasta evenly and let it heat through for 1-2 minutes.

6. Season and Garnish:

·   Taste and adjust the seasoning with salt, black pepper, and additional red pepper flakes if desired.

7. Serve:

·   Serve the shrimp linguini immediately, garnished with grated Parmesan cheese if you like. This dish pairs won- derfully with a simple green salad or crusty bread.

8. Enjoy:

·   Enjoy your homemade shrimp linguini, a delightful com- bination of succulent shrimp, creamy lemony sauce, and perfectly cooked linguini pasta.

Baked Shrimp with Tomatoes and Feta Recipe

Ingredients:

- 1 pound large shrimp, peeled and deveined
- 2 tablespoons olive oil
- 4 cloves garlic, minced
- 1 can (14 ounces) diced tomatoes, drained
- 1/2 cup crumbled feta cheese
- 2 tablespoons fresh parsley, chopped
- 1 teaspoon dried oregano
- 1/2 teaspoon dried basil
- 1/4 teaspoon red pepper flakes (adjust to taste, for spiciness)
- Salt and black pepper, to taste
- Crusty bread or cooked orzo, for serving
- Lemon wedges, for garnish (optional)

Instructions:

1. Preheat the Oven:
- Preheat your oven to 375°F (190°C).
2. Sauté the Shrimp:
- In a large ovenproof skillet, heat the olive oil over medium- high heat. Add the minced garlic and sauté for about 30 seconds until fragrant.
- Add the peeled and deveined shrimp to the skillet and cook for 1-2 minutes per side, just until they start to turn pink. Remove the shrimp from the skillet and set them aside.
3. Prepare the Tomato Sauce:
- In the same skillet, add the drained diced tomatoes, dried oregano, dried basil, red pepper flakes, salt, and black pepper. Stir to combine.
4. Bake with Shrimp and Feta:
- Return the cooked shrimp to the skillet, arranging them evenly in the tomato sauce.
- Sprinkle the crumbled feta cheese over the shrimp and tomato mixture.
5. Bake in the Oven:
- Place the skillet in the preheated oven and bake for about 15-20 minutes or until the shrimp are fully cooked and the cheese is melted and bubbly. The exact baking time may vary depending on

the size of your shrimp, so keep an eye on them.

6. Garnish and Serve:

·   Remove the skillet from the oven and sprinkle chopped fresh parsley over the baked shrimp.

·   Serve the baked shrimp with tomatoes and feta hot, straight from the skillet. It's delicious when served with crusty bread for dipping into the flavorful sauce. Alternatively, you can serve it over cooked orzo for a heartier meal.

7. Enjoy:

·   Enjoy your Baked Shrimp with Tomatoes and Feta, a delight- ful dish bursting with Mediterranean flavors and the perfect balance of juicy shrimp, tangy tomatoes, and creamy feta cheese. Garnish with lemon wedges if you like for an extra zesty kick.

On the Side

Baked Potato Recipe

Prep Time: 5 minutes | Cook Time: 60-75 minutes | Total Time: 65-80 minutes

Servings: 4

Ingredients:

- 4 large russet potatoes (choose potatoes of similar size)
- 2 tablespoons olive oil
- Salt, to taste
- Black pepper, to taste
- Optional toppings: butter, sour cream, shredded cheese, chives, bacon bits, or your favorite toppings

Instructions:

1. Preheat the Oven:
- Preheat your oven to 375°F (190°C).

2. Prepare the Potatoes:
- Wash and scrub the russet potatoes thoroughly under run- ning water to remove any dirt. Pat them dry with a paper towel.

3. Poke the Potatoes:
- Use a fork to prick the potatoes several times on all sides. This helps steam escape during baking.

4. Coat with Olive Oil and Season:
- Rub each potato with olive oil, ensuring they are well-coated. This will help the skin become crispy during baking.
- Season each potato generously with salt and black pepper.

5. Bake the Potatoes:
- Place the seasoned potatoes directly on the oven rack or on a baking sheet lined with foil or parch- ment paper. This will catch any drips and make cleanup easier.
- Bake for 60-75 minutes, or until the potatoes are tender when pierced with a fork or skewer. The exact cooking time depends on the size and type of potatoes, so check them periodically.

6. Check for Doneness:
- To ensure the potatoes are fully cooked, insert a fork or skewer into the center. It should go in easily without resistance.

7. Remove from Oven:
- Once the potatoes are done, remove them from the oven. Be careful, as they will be hot.

8. Serve and Add Toppings:

· Slice each baked potato lengthwise and fluff the insides with a fork.

· Add your favorite toppings, such as butter, sour cream, shredded cheese, chives, bacon bits, or any other toppings you prefer.

9. Enjoy:

· Serve the baked potatoes hot as a side dish or as a meal on their own.

Baked potatoes are a versatile and satisfying dish that can be customized with your favorite toppings. They make a great side dish for a variety of meals or a simple and comforting meal on their own.

Creamy Mashed Potatoes Recipe

Prep Time: 15 minutes | Cook Time: 20-25 minutes | Total Time: 35-40 minutes

Servings: 4-6

Ingredients:

- 2 pounds (about 4 large) russet potatoes, peeled and cut into 1-inch cubes
- 4 cups water
- 1 teaspoon salt, for boiling
- 1/2 cup unsalted butter (1 stick)
- 1 cup whole milk or half-and-half, warmed
- Salt and white pepper, to taste
- Chopped fresh parsley or chives for garnish (optional)

Instructions:

1. Boil the Potatoes:
- Place the peeled and cubed potatoes in a large pot and cover them with cold water. Add 1 teaspoon of salt to the water.
- Bring the water to a boil over high heat, then reduce the heat to medium-high and simmer the potatoes for about 20-25 minutes or until they are fork-tender. You should be able to easily pierce a potato cube with a fork.

2. Drain the Potatoes:
- Once the potatoes are cooked, drain them in a colander and let them sit for a minute to allow excess moisture to evaporate.

3. Mash the Potatoes:
- Return the drained potatoes to the pot. Use a potato masher or a hand mixer to mash the potatoes until they are mostly smooth. Some small lumps are okay if you prefer a rustic texture.

4. Add Butter:
- Cut the butter into small pieces and add it to the mashed potatoes. Stir until the butter is fully melted and incorpo- rated.

5. Add Warm Milk:
- Gradually pour in the warm milk or half-and-half while continuing to mix the potatoes. This will make them creamy and smooth.

6. Season:
- Season the mashed potatoes with salt and white pepper to taste. Adjust the seasoning according to your preference.

7. Final Mix:

· Give the mashed potatoes one final mix to ensure every- thing is well combined and creamy. Taste and adjust the seasonings if needed.

8. Garnish and Serve:

· Transfer the creamy mashed potatoes to a serving dish.

· If desired, garnish with chopped fresh parsley or chives for a burst of color and added flavor.

9. Serve Hot:

· Serve your homemade creamy mashed potatoes hot as a delicious side dish that pairs perfectly with a variety of main courses.

These creamy mashed potatoes are a classic comfort food and a perfect accompaniment to roast chicken, steak, or any of your favorite main dishes. Enjoy!

Roasted Potato Wedges

Ingredients:

· 4 large russet or Yukon Gold potatoes, scrubbed and cut into wedges

· 2 tablespoons olive oil

· 2 teaspoons Old Bay seasoning (adjust to taste)

· Salt and black pepper, to taste

· Fresh parsley or chives, chopped, for garnish (optional)

Instructions:

1. Preheat the Oven:

· Preheat your oven to 425°F (220°C). Place a rimmed baking sheet in the oven to heat up while you prepare the potatoes.

2. Prepare the Potatoes:

· Scrub the potatoes well and cut them into wedges. You can leave the skin on for extra texture and flavor.

3. Season the Potatoes:

· In a large bowl, combine the potato wedges, olive oil, Old Bay seasoning, garlic powder, onion powder, paprika, salt, and black pepper. Toss to coat the potatoes evenly with the seasoning mixture.

4. Arrange on the Baking Sheet:

· Carefully remove the hot baking sheet from the oven and place the seasoned potato wedges in a single layer. Make sure they are spaced apart to allow for even roasting.

5. Roast in the Oven:

· Roast the potato wedges in the preheated oven for about 30-35 minutes, or until they are golden brown and crispy on the outside, and tender on the inside. Be sure to flip them once halfway through the roasting time for even cooking.

6. Garnish and Serve:

· Remove the roasted potato wedges from the oven and transfer them to a serving platter. If desired, garnish with chopped fresh parsley or chives.

7. Enjoy:

· Serve your Roasted Potato Wedges with Bay Seasoning as a delicious side dish or snack. They are flavorful, crispy, and have a hint of the classic Old Bay seasoning that adds a unique twist to traditional roasted potatoes.

Creamy Broccoli and Cheese Rice Recipe

Ingredients:

- 1 cup long-grain white rice
- 2 cups chicken or vegetable broth
- 1 1/2 cups fresh broccoli florets (or frozen broccoli, thawed)
- 1 cup shredded cheddar cheese
- 2 tablespoons butter
- 1/2 cup diced onion
- 2 cloves garlic, minced
- Salt and black pepper, to taste
- Optional garnish: Chopped fresh parsley or chives

Instructions:

1. Cook the Rice:
- In a medium-sized saucepan, combine the rice and chicken or vegetable broth. Bring to a boil, then reduce the heat to low, cover, and simmer for about 15-18 minutes, or until the rice is tender and has absorbed most of the liquid. Remove from heat and fluff with a fork.

2. Steam the Broccoli:
- While the rice is cooking, place the fresh broccoli florets in a microwave-safe dish with a lid. Add a couple of tablespoons of water, cover with the lid, and microwave on high for 2-3 minutes, or until the broccoli is bright green and slightly tender. If using frozen broccoli, you can simply thaw it.

3. Sauté the Onion and Garlic:
- In a large skillet, melt the butter over medium heat. Add the diced onion and minced garlic. Sauté for about 2-3 minutes, or until the onion becomes translucent and fragrant.

4. Combine Rice, Broccoli, and Cheese:
- Add the cooked rice, steamed broccoli, and shredded ched- dar cheese to the skillet with the sautéed onion and garlic. Stir well to combine and allow the cheese to melt and coat the rice and broccoli evenly.

5. Season:
- Season the dish with salt and black pepper to taste. Adjust the seasoning according to your preference.

6. Garnish and Serve:
- If desired, garnish your Creamy Broccoli and Cheese Rice with chopped fresh parsley or chives for added color and flavor.

7. Enjoy:
- Serve your delicious Creamy Broccoli and Cheese Rice as a side dish or a comforting vegetarian meal. The creamy cheese complements the tender broccoli and fluffy rice, creating a delightful combination of flavors and textures.

Spanish Rice Recipe

Ingredients:

- · 1 cup long-grain white rice
- · 2 tablespoons vegetable oil
- · 1 small onion, finely chopped
- · 1 bell pepper, diced (any color you prefer)
- · 2 cloves garlic, minced
- · 1 can (14 ounces) diced tomatoes, undrained
- · 1 1/2 cups chicken or vegetable broth
- · 1 teaspoon ground cumin
- · 1 teaspoon chili powder
- · 1/2 teaspoon paprika
- · Salt and black pepper, to taste
- · Optional garnish: Fresh chopped cilantro or parsley

Instructions:

1. Rinse and Toast the Rice:
- · Rinse the rice under cold water until the water runs clear. Drain well.
- · In a large skillet or saucepan, heat the vegetable oil over medium heat. Add the rinsed rice and toast it, stirring frequently, until it becomes slightly translucent and starts to smell nutty. This should take about 3-5 minutes.

2. Sauté the Vegetables:
- · Add the finely chopped onion and diced bell pepper to the skillet with the toasted rice. Sauté for about 2-3 minutes, or until the vegetables begin to soften.
- · Stir in the minced garlic and sauté for an additional 30 seconds until fragrant.
- · Add Tomatoes and Seasonings:
- · Pour in the can of diced tomatoes, including the liquid. Stir to combine.
- · Add the ground cumin, chili powder, paprika, salt, and black pepper. Stir well to distribute the seasonings evenly.

3. Simmer with Broth:
- · Pour in the chicken or vegetable broth and stir everything together.

4. Simmer and Cover:
- · Bring the mixture to a boil, then reduce the heat to low. Cover the skillet with a tight-fitting lid.

5. Simmer:

- Let the rice simmer on low heat for about 15-20 minutes, or until the liquid is absorbed, and the rice is tender. Avoid opening the lid during this time to prevent steam from escaping.

6. Fluff and Rest:

- Once the rice is cooked, remove the skillet from the heat and let it sit, covered, for an additional 5-10 minutes. This resting time allows the rice to absorb any remaining moisture and become fluffy.

7. Garnish and Serve:

- Fluff the Spanish rice with a fork to separate the grains. If desired, garnish with fresh chopped cilantro or parsley for added flavor and color.

8. Enjoy:

- Serve your homemade Spanish Rice as a flavorful side dish alongside your favorite Mexican or Spanish-inspired main courses. It's a tasty complement to dishes like enchiladas, tacos, grilled chicken, or beef.

Ranch Baked Beans Recipe

Ingredients

- · 2 cans (each 15 ounces) navy or great northern beans, drained and rinsed
- · 1 medium onion, finely chopped
- · 1/2 green bell pepper, finely chopped
- · 2 cloves garlic, minced
- · 1 cup barbecue sauce
- · 1/2 cup ranch dressing
- · 1/4 cup brown sugar
- · 2 tablespoons molasses
- · 1 tablespoon Worcestershire sauce
- · 1 teaspoon smoked paprika
- · 1 teaspoon dry mustard powder
- · Salt and black pepper, to taste
- · Optional: 4 slices of bacon, cooked and crumbled (for garnish)
- · Optional: Fresh parsley, chopped (for garnish)

Instructions

1. Preheat the Oven:
- · Preheat your oven to 350°F (175°C).
2. Prepare the Bean Mixture:
- · In a large mixing bowl, combine the drained and rinsed beans, chopped onion, green bell pepper, and minced garlic.
- · In another bowl, whisk together the barbecue sauce, ranch dressing, brown sugar, molasses, Worcestershire sauce, smoked paprika, and mustard powder until well blended.
- · Pour the sauce mixture over the beans and stir until the beans are evenly coated.
- · Season with salt and black pepper to taste.
3. Bake the Beans:
- · Transfer the bean mixture to a greased baking dish.
- · Cover the dish with aluminum foil and bake in the preheated oven for about 45 minutes.
- · After 45 minutes, remove the foil and continue to bake for another 15 minutes, or until the beans are bubbly and the top is slightly caramelized.

4. Garnish and Serve:

- If using, sprinkle the cooked, crumbled bacon over the top of the baked beans.

- Garnish with chopped fresh parsley for a touch of color and freshness.

- Serve hot as a delicious side dish, perfect for barbecues, picnics, or as a hearty accompaniment to any meal.

5. Enjoy!

- These ranch baked beans offer a delightful twist on the classic baked beans recipe, combining the tangy flavor of ranch with the sweet and smoky taste of barbecue sauce.

-

This recipe is great for those who love the traditional flavor of baked beans but are looking for something a bit different. The addition of ranch dressing adds a creamy, tangy dimension that pairs wonderfully with the beans' nat

Glazed Carrots Recipe

Ingredients

- 1 pound carrots, peeled and sliced into 1/4 inch thick rounds
- 3 tablespoons butter
- 3 tablespoons brown sugar
- 1/2 cup orange juice
- Salt and pepper, to taste
- Optional: 1/2 teaspoon ground cinnamon or nutmeg for added flavor
- Optional: Chopped parsley or thyme for garnish

Instructions

1. Prepare the Carrots:
- If using whole carrots, peel them and slice into rounds about 1/4 inch thick. For uniform cooking, try to keep the slices consistently sized.
2. Cook the Carrots:
- In a large skillet, melt the butter over medium heat.
- Add the sliced carrots to the skillet. Cook for about 4-5 minutes, stirring occasionally, until they start to soften.
3. Add Sweetness and Flavor:
- Sprinkle the brown sugar over the carrots and pour in the orange juice.
- If using, add the ground cinnamon or nutmeg. This step is optional but adds a nice warmth to the dish.
- Season with salt and pepper to taste.
- Stir everything together, ensuring the carrots are well coated.
4. Glaze the Carrots:
- Reduce the heat to medium-low. Allow the carrots to simmer in the sauce for about 10-15 minutes, or until the carrots are tender and the sauce has reduced to a glaze.
- Stir occasionally to ensure the carrots are evenly coated and the sauce doesn't burn.
5. Finish and Serve:
- Once the carrots are tender and glazed, check the seasoning and adjust if necessary.
- Remove from heat. If desired, garnish with chopped parsley or thyme for a fresh, herby touch.

6. Enjoy!

· Serve the glazed carrots hot as a delicious and attractive side dish. They pair wonderfully with a variety of main courses, from roasts to grilled meats.

This Glazed Carrots recipe offers a delightful combination of sweetness and tenderness, making it a favorite side dish for both everyday meals and special occasions. The gentle caramelization from the brown sugar and the citrusy note from the orange juice bring out the natural flavors of the carrots beautifully.

Steamed Corn on the Cob Recipe

Prep Time: 5 minutes | Cook Time: 7-10 minutes | Total Time: 12-15 minutes

Serving Size: Varies (1 ear of corn per person)

Ingredients:

- Fresh ears of corn (as many as you need)
- Butter (optional)
- Salt (optional)
- Fresh herbs for garnish (optional, such as parsley or cilantro)

Instructions:

1. Prepare the Corn:

- Husk the corn by removing the outer green leaves and silk threads. Rinse the corn under cold water to clean off any remaining silk.

2. Prepare Your Steamer:

- Fill a large pot with about two inches of water. Bring the water to a boil. If you have a steamer basket, place it in the pot. If not, you can lay the corn directly in the pot, but it should not be submerged in water.

3. Steam the Corn:

- Place the ears of corn in the steamer
- basket or directly in the pot. Cover the pot with a lid. Steam the corn for about 7 to 10 minutes. The exact time will depend on the size of the corn and how tender you like it.

4. Check for Doneness:

- To check if the corn is done, pierce it with a fork. The kernels should be tender and juicy.

5. Serve:

- Remove the corn from the steamer and place it on a serving dish. If desired, brush each ear with butter and sprinkle with salt. You can also add other seasonings or fresh herbs.

6. Enjoy:

- Serve the steamed corn on the cob while it's warm.

Tips:

- · Avoid over-steaming as it can make the corn tough and lose its sweet flavor.

- · For added flavor, you can add herbs or a clove of garlic to the steaming water.

- · Steamed corn on the cob pairs well with a variety of dishes, especially grilled meats or summer salads.

- · For a twist, try rubbing the cooked corn with lime juice and a sprinkle of chili powder or paprika.

Steamed corn on the cob is a simple, healthy, and delicious way to enjoy fresh corn. It retains more nutrients than boiling and brings out the natural sweetness of the corn. This recipe is straightforward and perfect for a quick side dish.

Roasted Brussels Sprouts Recipe

Ingredients

- 1 1/2 pounds Brussels sprouts
- 3 tablespoons olive oil
- 3/4 teaspoon kosher salt
- 1/2 teaspoon freshly ground black pepper
- Optional: 2 cloves of garlic, minced (for extra flavor)
- Optional: 1/2 teaspoon red pepper flakes (for a spicy kick)
- Optional garnishes: grated Parmesan cheese, balsamic glaze, or lemon zest

Instructions

1. Preheat the Oven:
- Preheat your oven to 400°F (205°C). This high temperature is key for getting crispy, caramelized Brussels sprouts.
2. Prepare the Brussels Sprouts:
- Rinse the Brussels sprouts under cold water and pat them dry with paper towels.
- Trim off the stem ends and remove any yellow or damaged outer leaves.
- Cut each Brussels sprout in half lengthwise. If they are particularly large, you can cut them into quarters.
3. Season the Brussels Sprouts:
- In a large mixing bowl, toss the Brussels sprouts with olive oil, ensuring they are well coated.
- Add salt and black pepper, and toss again. If using, also add minced garlic and red pepper flakes at this stage.
4. Roast the Brussels Sprouts:
- Spread the Brussels sprouts out in an even layer on a baking sheet. Make sure they are not too crowded; otherwise, they will steam rather than roast.
- Place in the oven and roast for 20-25 minutes. Halfway through the cooking time, give the pan a good shake or stir the Brussels sprouts to ensure even browning.
5. Finish and Serve:
- The Brussels sprouts are done when they are deeply golden and crispy on the outside and tender on the inside.
- Taste and adjust seasoning, if necessary.
- If desired, sprinkle with grated Parmesan cheese, drizzle with balsamic glaze, or add a zest of lemon before serving.

6. Enjoy!

- Serve the roasted Brussels sprouts hot as a delicious side dish. They are perfect for a regular family dinner or special enough for a holiday meal.

This roasted Brussels sprouts recipe is a simple and tasty way to enjoy this nutritious vegetable. The high heat of the oven brings out their natural sweetness and creates a delightful crispy texture.

Grilled Asparagus Recipe

Ingredients

- · 1 pound fresh asparagus spears, trimmed
- · 2 tablespoons olive oil
- · Salt, to taste
- · Black pepper, to taste
- · 1 lemon, halved (for juice)
- · Optional: Grated Parmesan cheese or lemon zest for garnish

Instructions

1. Preheat the Grill:
- · Preheat your grill to medium-high heat (about 400°F or 200°C). Ensure the grill grates are clean to prevent sticking.
2. Prepare the Asparagus:
- · Rinse the asparagus spears under cold water and pat them dry with paper towels.
- · Trim off the tough ends of the asparagus. This is usually about 1-2 inches from the bottom.
3. Season the Asparagus:
- · Place the trimmed asparagus in a large bowl or baking dish.
- · Drizzle with olive oil and toss to ensure all the spears are evenly coated.
- · Season with salt and freshly ground black pepper, tossing again to distribute the seasonings.
4. Grill the Asparagus:
- · Arrange the asparagus spears on the grill in a single layer. If your grates are wide, you might want to use a grill basket or skewer the asparagus to prevent them from falling through.
- · Grill the asparagus for 3-4 minutes per side, turning oc- casionally. The exact cooking time will depend on the thickness of the spears.
- · The asparagus should be tender and lightly charred when done.
5. Finish and Serve:
- · Transfer the grilled asparagus to a serving platter.
- · Squeeze fresh lemon juice over the grilled spears to add a bright, citrusy flavor.
- · If desired, sprinkle with grated Parmesan cheese or lemon zest for extra flavor.
6. Enjoy!
- · Serve the grilled asparagus hot as a delightful side dish that pairs well with a variety of main courses.

This simple yet elegant grilled asparagus dish is perfect for a summer barbecue or as a healthy side to your main meal, offering a delicious way to enjoy this nutritious vegetable.

Steamed Vegetables Recipe

Prep Time: 10 minutes | Cook Time: 5-15 minutes (depending on the vegetable) | Total Time: 15-25 minutes

Servings: 4

Ingredients:

- Assorted vegetables (e.g., broccoli, cauliflower, carrots, green beans, asparagus, zucchini, frozen peas)
- Water
- Salt (optional)
- Butter or olive oil (optional, for seasoning)
- Lemon juice (optional, for flavor)

Equipment:

- Steamer basket or microwave-safe steaming dish with lid
- Pot with a tight-fitting lid (if using stovetop method)
- Microwave (if using microwave method)

Instructions:

1. Choose and Prepare Your Vegetables:
- Wash and prepare your vegetables by trimming, peeling, or cutting them into bite-sized pieces, as desired.
2. Set Up Your Steaming Equipment:
- There are two common methods for steaming vegetables: stovetop and microwave. Choose the one that suits you best:
3. Stovetop Method:
- Fill a pot with a few inches of water and insert a steamer basket. Make sure the water doesn't touch the bottom of the basket.
- Place the prepared vegetables in the steamer basket.
4. Microwave Method:
- Place the prepared vegetables in a microwave-safe steaming dish with a lid.
5. Steam the Vegetables:

    Stovetop Method:
- Cover the pot with a tight-fitting lid and bring the water to a boil over medium-high heat.
- Reduce the heat to medium-low to maintain a gentle sim- mer.
- Steam the vegetables for 3-15 minutes, depending on the type and size of the vegetables:

- Broccoli, cauliflower, asparagus: 3-5 minutes
- Carrots, green beans: 5-7 minutes
- Zucchini, summer squash: 4-6 minutes
- Check for doneness by poking a fork or knife into the vegetables; they should be tender but still crisp. Avoid overcooking, as the vegetables can become mushy.

Microwave Method:

- Add a few tablespoons of water to the bottom of the steaming dish.
- Cover the dish with the lid.
- Microwave on high for 2-6 minutes, depending on the type and quantity of vegetables.
- Check for doneness by poking a fork or knife into the vegetables. They should be tender but still crisp.

6. Season and Serve:

- Once the vegetables are done, season them with salt, if desired, and add a drizzle of melted butter or olive oil for extra flavor.
- You can also squeeze fresh lemon juice over the steamed vegetables for a bright, zesty touch.

7. Enjoy:

- Serve your steamed vegetables as a healthy side dish along- side your favorite main course.

Steaming vegetables is a quick and healthy cooking method that preserves their color, flavor, and nutrients. Customize your steamed vegetables with your preferred seasonings and enjoy their natural goodness.

Creamy Southern Coleslaw Recipe

Prep Time: 15 minutes | Chill Time: 1-2 hours | Total Time: 1 hour and 15 minutes

Servings: 6-8

Ingredients:

- · For the Coleslaw:
- · 1 medium-sized green cabbage, finely shredded (about 6 cups)
- · 2 medium-sized carrots, grated
- · 1/2 cup sweet onion, finely chopped (optional)
- · 1/4 cup fresh parsley, finely chopped (optional)

For the Dressing:

- · 1 cup mayonnaise
- · 1/4 cup buttermilk
- · 2 tablespoons apple cider vinegar
- · 2 tablespoons granulated sugar
- · 1 tablespoon Dijon mustard
- · 1 teaspoon celery seed
- · 1/2 teaspoon salt (adjust to taste)
- · 1/4 teaspoon black pepper (adjust to taste)

Instructions:

1. Prepare the Coleslaw:
- · Start by finely shredding the green cabbage. You can use a sharp knife or a food processor with a shredding attachment.
- · Grate the carrots and finely chop the sweet onion and fresh parsley.
2. Mix the Dressing:
- · In a separate mixing bowl, whisk together the mayonnaise, buttermilk, apple cider vinegar, granulated sugar, Dijon mustard, celery seed, salt, and black pepper. Mix until the dressing is smooth and well combined.
3. Combine Coleslaw and Dressing:
- · In a large mixing bowl, combine the shredded cabbage, grated carrots, chopped sweet onion (if using), and chopped fresh parsley (if using).
- · Pour the creamy dressing over the coleslaw mixture.

4. Toss and Chill:

· Gently toss the coleslaw and dressing together until all the vegetables are well coated.

· Cover the bowl with plastic wrap or a lid and refrigerate for at least 1-2 hours. This chilling time allows the flavors to meld and the coleslaw to become more flavorful.

5. Serve:

· Before serving, give the coleslaw a final toss to ensure the dressing is evenly distributed.

· Serve your creamy Southern coleslaw as a side dish at your next barbecue, picnic, or family gathering.

This creamy Southern coleslaw is the perfect balance of tangy and sweet, making it a delightful side dish that complements grilled meats, sandwiches, and other Southern classics. Enjoy its refreshing crunch and flavor!

Fettuccine Alfredo Recipe

Prep Time: 5 minutes | Cook Time: 15 minutes | Total Time: 20 minutes

Servings: 4

Ingredients:

- 12 ounces fettuccine pasta
- 1/2 cup (1 stick) unsalted butter
- 1 cup heavy cream
- 4 ounces cream cheese, cut into cubes
- 1 cup grated Parmesan cheese
- 1 teaspoon garlic powder
- Salt and black pepper, to taste
- Fresh parsley, chopped, for garnish (optional)

Instructions:

1. Cook the Pasta:
- Bring a large pot of salted water to a boil. Add the fettuccine pasta and cook according to package instructions until al dente. Drain the pasta and set it aside.

2. Prepare the Alfredo Sauce:
- In a large skillet or saucepan, melt the unsalted butter over medium heat.
- Stir in the heavy cream and bring it to a simmer. Let it cook for a couple of minutes, allowing it to thicken slightly.

3. Add Cream Cheese and Parmesan:
- Reduce the heat to low. Stir in the cubed cream cheese and grated Parmesan cheese. Continue to stir until the cheeses have melted and the sauce is smooth and creamy.

4. Season:
- Stir in the garlic powder, salt, and black pepper, adjusting to taste.

5. Combine Pasta and Sauce:
- Return the drained fettuccine pasta to the pot. Pour the creamy Alfredo sauce over the pasta.

6. Toss and Heat:
- Toss the pasta and sauce together until the pasta is well coated and heated through. You can add a little extra cream or pasta cooking water if the sauce is too thick.

7. Serve:
- Serve the cream cheese fettuccine Alfredo hot, garnished with chopped fresh parsley if desired.

8. Enjoy:

- Enjoy this rich and creamy fettuccine Alfredo with cream cheese as a comforting and indulgent main course.

This variation of fettuccine Alfredo with cream cheese adds a delightful tanginess and creaminess to the classic recipe. It's a perfect choice for a cozy and satisfying meal.

Creamy Macaroni and Cheese Recipe

Prep Time: 10 minutes | Cook Time: 20 minutes | Total Time: 30 minutes

Servings: 6

Ingredients:

- 8 ounces (about 2 cups) elbow macaroni or pasta of your choice
- 1/4 cup (1/2 stick) unsalted butter
- 1/4 cup all-purpose flour
- 2 cups whole milk
- 1 cup heavy cream
- 2 cups shredded sharp cheddar cheese
- 1 cup shredded mozzarella cheese
- 1/2 cup grated Parmesan cheese
- 1/2 teaspoon salt, or to taste
- 1/4 teaspoon black pepper, or to taste
- 1/4 teaspoon paprika (optional, for color and flavor)
- 1/4 teaspoon garlic powder (optional)
- 1/4 teaspoon onion powder (optional)
- 1/4 teaspoon mustard powder (optional)

Instructions:

1. Cook the Pasta:

- Bring a large pot of salted water to a boil. Add the elbow macaroni and cook according to the package instructions until al dente. Drain and set aside.

2. Prepare the Cheese Sauce:

- In a large saucepan, melt the unsalted butter over medium heat.
- Stir in the all-purpose flour and cook for about 1-2 minutes, stirring constantly until the mixture turns a light golden color and begins to smell nutty.
- Gradually whisk in the whole milk and heavy cream. Con- tinue to whisk until the mixture is smooth and begins to thicken, about 5-7 minutes.

3. Add the Cheeses:

- Reduce the heat to low and add the shredded sharp cheddar cheese, shredded mozzarella cheese, and grated Parmesan cheese. Stir until the cheeses are completely melted and the sauce is smooth and creamy.

4. Season the Sauce:

· Season the cheese sauce with salt, black pepper, paprika, garlic powder, onion powder, and mustard powder (if using). Adjust the seasoning to your taste.

5. Combine the Pasta and Cheese Sauce:

· Add the cooked and drained elbow macaroni to the cheese sauce. Stir to coat the pasta evenly with the creamy cheese sauce.

6. Serve:

· Serve the creamy macaroni and cheese hot, garnished with extra grated Parmesan cheese and a sprinkle of paprika if desired.

7. Enjoy:

· Enjoy your homemade macaroni and cheese as a comforting and satisfying meal.

This classic macaroni and cheese recipe is rich, creamy, and full of cheesy goodness. It's perfect as a side dish or a main course, and you can customize it with your favorite mix of cheeses for a unique twist.

Classic Cornbread Recipe

Ingredients:

- 1 cup all-purpose flour
- 1 cup yellow cornmeal
- 1/4 cup white sugar
- 1 tablespoon baking powder
- 1/2 teaspoon salt
- 1 cup milk
- 1/3 cup vegetable oil
- 1 large egg

Instructions:

1. Preheat Oven and Prepare Pan:
- Preheat your oven to 400°F (200°C).
- Grease an 8-inch square baking pan or line it with parch- ment paper.
2. Combine Dry Ingredients:
- In a large bowl, mix together the flour, cornmeal, sugar, baking powder, and salt.
3. Mix Wet Ingredients:
- In a separate bowl, beat together the milk, vegetable oil, and egg.
4. Combine Wet and Dry Ingredients:
- Add the wet ingredients to the dry ingredients and stir until just combined. Be careful not to over-mix, as this can make the cornbread tough.
5. Pour Batter into Pan:
- Pour the batter into the prepared baking pan and smooth the top with a spatula.
6. Bake the Cornbread:
- Bake in the preheated oven for 20 to 25 minutes, or until a toothpick inserted into the center comes out clean.
7. Cool and Serve:
- Allow the cornbread to cool in the pan for a few minutes before cutting.
- Serve warm with butter, honey, or your favorite toppings.

8. Tips:

· For a richer flavor, substitute buttermilk for regular milk.

· Add-ins like shredded cheese, chopped jalapeños, or corn kernels can be folded into the batter for extra flavor.

· Cornbread can be stored in an airtight container at room temperature for up to 2 days or refrigerated for longer storage.

Enjoy your homemade cornbread! It's perfect as a side for soups, chili, or enjoyed on its own as a tasty snack.

Garlic Bread Recipe

Prep Time: 10 minutes | Cook Time: 10 minutes | Total Time: 20 minutes

Servings: 4-6

Ingredients:

- 1 loaf of Italian bread or French bread
- 1/2 cup (1 stick) unsalted butter, at room temperature
- 4-6 cloves garlic, minced
- 2 tablespoons fresh parsley, finely chopped
- Salt and black pepper, to taste
- Grated Parmesan cheese (optional, for garnish)

Instructions:

1. Preheat the Oven:
- Preheat your oven to 375°F (190°C).
2. Slice the Bread:
- Cut the Italian or French bread in half horizontally, creating two long halves.
3. Prepare the Garlic Butter Mixture:
- In a mixing bowl, combine the softened unsalted butter, minced garlic, finely chopped fresh parsley, a pinch of salt, and a dash of black pepper. Mix well until all the ingredients are thoroughly combined.
4. Spread the Garlic Butter:
- Spread the garlic butter mixture evenly over the cut sides of both halves of the bread. Be generous with the spread to ensure every bite is flavorful.
5. Reassemble the Bread:
- Place the two halves of the bread back together, creating a whole loaf.
6. Wrap in Foil:
- Wrap the garlic bread loaf in aluminum foil, leaving the top slightly open to allow steam to escape while baking.
7. Bake:
- Place the wrapped garlic bread loaf on a baking sheet and bake in the preheated oven for about 10 minutes, or until the bread is heated through, the butter is melted, and the edges are slightly crispy.

8. Optional Broil (for Crispy Top):

- If you prefer a crispier top, carefully open the foil and broil the garlic bread under the broiler for an additional 1-2 minutes, watching closely to avoid burning. This step is optional but adds a nice texture to the bread.

9. Slice and Garnish:

- Remove the garlic bread from the oven and carefully unwrap it from the foil.

- Optionally, sprinkle grated Parmesan cheese over the hot garlic bread for extra flavor and garnish.

10. Serve:

- Slice the garlic bread into individual portions and serve it hot as a delicious side dish or appetizer.

Enjoy your homemade garlic bread, with its rich garlic and buttery flavor, as a perfect complement to pasta dishes, soups, salads, or as an appetizer for any meal!

Homemade Biscuits Recipe

Prep Time: 15 minutes | Cook Time: 12-15 minutes | Total Time: 30 minutes

Servings: 12 biscuits

Ingredients:

- 2 cups all-purpose flour
- 1 tablespoon baking powder
- 1 teaspoon sugar
- 1/2 teaspoon salt
- 1/2 cup (1 stick) cold unsalted butter, cubed
- 3/4 cup cold buttermilk
- Additional buttermilk or melted butter for brushing (op- tional)

Instructions:

1. Preheat the Oven:
- Preheat your oven to 450°F (230°C). Line a baking sheet with parchment paper or lightly grease it.
2. Combine Dry Ingredients:
- In a large mixing bowl, whisk together the all-purpose flour, baking powder, sugar, and salt.
3. Cut in the Butter:
- Add the cold, cubed butter to the dry ingredients. Using a pastry cutter or your fingers, work the butter into the flour mixture until it resembles coarse crumbs. The butter pieces should be about the size of small peas.
4. Add the Buttermilk:
- Pour the cold buttermilk over the flour mixture. Stir gently with a fork or a spatula until the dough comes together. Be careful not to overmix; it's okay if there are a few dry spots.
5. Knead the Dough:
- Turn the dough out onto a lightly floured surface. Gently knead it a few times, just until it comes together and is no longer sticky.
6. Roll and Cut:
- Roll the dough out to a thickness of about 1/2 to 3/4 inch. Using a round biscuit cutter or the rim of a glass, cut out biscuits. Press straight down without twisting the cutter to ensure the biscuits rise evenly.
7. Place on Baking Sheet:
- Transfer the cut biscuits to the prepared baking sheet, placing them close together, but not touching.

8. Bake:

·   Place the baking sheet in the preheated oven and bake for 12-15 minutes, or until the biscuits are golden brown on top and cooked through. They should sound hollow when tapped on the bottom.

9. Optional Brushing:

·   If desired, brush the hot biscuits with melted butter for added flavor and a shiny finish.

10. Serve Warm:

·   Serve your homemade biscuits warm. They're great on their own, with butter, jam, honey, or as part of a breakfast sandwich.

Enjoy your freshly baked homemade biscuits — tender, flaky, and perfect for any meal or occasion!

Parmesan Garlic Knots Recipe

Ingredients

- · 1 pound pizza dough, store-bought or homemade
- · 4 tablespoons unsalted butter, melted
- · 3 cloves garlic, minced
- · 2 tablespoons freshly grated Parmesan cheese
- · 1 teaspoon garlic powder
- · 1 teaspoon dried oregano
- · 1/2 teaspoon dried parsley
- · 1/4 teaspoon salt
- · Optional: Red pepper flakes for a spicy kick
- · Optional: Fresh parsley, chopped, for garnish

Instructions

1. Prepare the Dough:
- · Let the pizza dough sit at room temperature for about 20 minutes, making it easier to work with.
- · Preheat your oven to 375°F (190°C). Line a baking sheet with parchment paper.
2. Form the Knots:
- · On a lightly floured surface, roll out the pizza dough into a rectangle, approximately 1/2 inch thick.
- · Cut the dough into 1-inch wide strips. Then tie each strip into a knot, tucking the ends underneath.
- · Place the knots on the prepared baking sheet, spaced slightly apart.
3. Make the Garlic Butter Mixture:
- · In a small bowl, combine melted butter, minced garlic, Parmesan cheese, garlic powder, oregano, parsley, and salt. Add red pepper flakes if desired.
- · Brush the garlic butter mixture generously over each knot.
4. Bake the Garlic Knots:
- · Bake in the preheated oven for 15-20 minutes or until they turn golden brown.
5. Serve:
- · If desired, brush the knots with a bit more garlic butter after baking.
- · Sprinkle with freshly chopped parsley for an added pop of color and freshness.
- · Serve warm as an appetizer or side dish, perfect with mari- nara sauce for dipping.

6. Enjoy!

• These garlic knots, bursting with buttery garlic flavor and a hint of Parmesan, are a delightful treat for any garlic bread enthusiast.

These Parmesan garlic knots are simple to make and are perfect for parties, gatherings, or as a tasty accompaniment to your favorite Italian dishes. The aromatic garlic and Parmesan butter give these knots a deliciously savory flavor that's hard to resist.

Desserts

Classic Chocolate Chip Cookie Recipe

Prep Time: 15 minutes | Cook Time: 10-12 minutes per batch | Total Time: 25-27 minutes
Yield: Approximately 24 cookies

Ingredients:

- 1 cup (2 sticks) unsalted butter, softened
- 3/4 cup granulated sugar
- 3/4 cup packed brown sugar (light or dark)
- 2 large eggs
- 1 teaspoon pure vanilla extract
- 2 1/4 cups all-purpose flour
- 1 teaspoon baking soda
- 1/2 teaspoon salt
- 2 cups semisweet chocolate chips
- 1 cup chopped nuts (optional)

Instructions:

1. Preheat the Oven:

- Preheat your oven to 375°F (190°C). Line baking sheets with parchment paper or silicone baking mats.

2. Cream the Butter and Sugars:

- In a large mixing bowl, cream together the softened butter, granulated sugar, and brown sugar until the mixture is light and fluffy. This should take about 2-3 minutes with an electric mixer.

3. Add Eggs and Vanilla:

- Beat in the eggs one at a time, ensuring each is fully incor- porated before adding the next. Mix in the vanilla extract.

4. Combine Dry Ingredients:

- In a separate bowl, whisk together the all-purpose flour, baking soda, and salt.

5. Gradually Add Dry Ingredients:

- Gradually add the dry ingredient mixture to the wet ingre- dients, mixing just until the dough comes together. Avoid overmixing, as this can make the cookies tough.

6. Add Chocolate Chips (and Nuts):

- Stir in the semisweet chocolate chips. If you like, you can also add chopped nuts of your choice, such as walnuts or pecans.

7. Form Cookie Dough Balls:

- Drop rounded tablespoons or use a cookie scoop to form cookie dough balls and place them on the prepared baking sheets, leaving some space between each for spreading.

8. Bake:

- Bake in the preheated oven for 10-12 minutes or until the edges are golden brown but the centers are still soft. The exact baking time may vary depending on your oven and the size of your cookies, so keep a close eye on them.

9. Cool on a Wire Rack:

- Allow the cookies to cool on the baking sheets for a few min- utes, then transfer them to wire racks to cool completely.

10. Enjoy:

- Once the cookies have cooled, enjoy them with a glass of milk or your favorite beverage.

Tips:

- For chewier cookies, slightly underbake them by removing them from the oven when they appear set but still soft in the center. They will continue to cook a bit as they cool on the baking sheets.

- Store leftover cookies in an airtight container at room temperature for up to several days. You can also freeze the cookie dough or baked cookies for longer storage.

These classic chocolate chip cookies are sure to be a hit with friends and family. Feel free to adjust the recipe to your taste, whether you prefer them with or without nuts or with different types of chocolate chips. Enjoy your homemade cookies!

Classic Peanut Butter Cookie Recipe

Prep Time: 15 minutes | Cook Time: 10-12 minutes per batch | Total Time: 25-27 minutes

Yield: Approximately 24 cookies

Ingredients:

- 1 cup (2 sticks) unsalted butter, softened
- 1 cup creamy peanut butter
- 1 cup granulated sugar
- 1 cup packed brown sugar (light or dark)
- 2 large eggs
- 1 teaspoon pure vanilla extract
- 2 1/2 cups all-purpose flour
- 1 1/2 teaspoons baking soda
- 1/2 teaspoon salt
- Additional granulated sugar for rolling (optional)
- Chocolate chips, chopped peanuts, or other toppings (op- tional)

Instructions:

1. Preheat the Oven:
- Preheat your oven to 350°F (175°C). Line baking sheets with parchment paper or silicone baking mats.
2. Cream Butter and Peanut Butter:
- In a large mixing bowl, cream together the softened butter and creamy peanut butter until well combined and creamy.
3. Add Sugars:
- Add the granulated sugar and packed brown sugar to the butter mixture. Continue to mix until the sugars are fully incorporated, and the mixture is smooth.
4. Add Eggs and Vanilla:
- Beat in the eggs one at a time, ensuring each is fully incorpo- rated before adding the next. Mix in the pure vanilla extract.
5. Combine Dry Ingredients:
- In a separate bowl, whisk together the all-purpose flour, baking soda, and salt.
6. Gradually Add Dry Ingredients:

· Gradually add the dry ingredient mixture to the wet ingre- dients, mixing just until the dough comes together. Avoid overmixing, as this can make the cookies tough.

7. Roll Cookie Dough Balls (Optional):

· If you like, you can roll portions of the cookie dough into small balls and place them on a plate or tray. You can later use a fork to create the classic crisscross pattern by pressing down on each cookie dough ball.

8. Place on Baking Sheets:

· Drop rounded tablespoons of cookie dough onto the pre- pared baking sheets, leaving some space between each cookie for spreading. If you've rolled the cookie dough balls, you can flatten them slightly with a fork, creating the crisscross pattern.

9. Add Toppings (Optional):

· If desired, you can press chocolate chips, chopped peanuts, or other toppings onto the tops of the cookies before baking.

10. Bake:

· Bake in the preheated oven for 10-12 minutes or until the edges are lightly golden but the centers are still slightly soft. The exact baking time may vary depending on your oven.

11. Cool on a Wire Rack:

· Allow the cookies to cool on the baking sheets for a few minutes, then transfer them to wire racks to cool completely.

12. Enjoy:

· Once the cookies have cooled, enjoy them with a glass of milk or your favorite beverage.

Tips:

· Store leftover cookies in an airtight container at room temperature for up to several days. You can also freeze the cookie dough or baked cookies for longer storage.

These classic peanut butter cookies are wonderfully nutty and delicious. Feel free to customize them with your favorite toppings or add-ins like chocolate chips or chopped peanuts. Enjoy your homemade peanut butter cookies!

Classic Sugar Cookie Recipe

Prep Time: 20 minutes | Chill Time: 2 hours | Cook Time: 8- 10 minutes per batch | Total Time: 2 hours 30 minutes

Yield: Approximately 24 cookies

Ingredients:

For the Cookies:

- 1 cup (2 sticks) unsalted butter, softened
- 1 1/2 cups granulated sugar
- 2 large eggs
- 2 teaspoons pure vanilla extract
- 3 cups all-purpose flour
- 1/2 teaspoon baking powder
- 1/2 teaspoon salt

For the Royal Icing (optional):

- 2 cups powdered sugar
- 1 1/2 tablespoons meringue powder
- 1/4 cup warm water
- Food coloring (optional)

Instructions:

1. Cream Butter and Sugar:

- In a large mixing bowl, cream together the softened butter and granulated sugar until the mixture is light and fluffy. This should take about 2-3 minutes.

2. Add Eggs and Vanilla:

- Beat in the eggs, one at a time, ensuring each is fully incorporated before adding the next. Mix in the pure vanilla extract.

3. Combine Dry Ingredients:

- In a separate bowl, whisk together the all-purpose flour, baking powder, and salt.

4. Gradually Add Dry Ingredients:

- Gradually add the dry ingredient mixture to the wet ingre- dients, mixing just until the dough comes together. Avoid overmixing, as this can make the cookies tough.

5. Form Cookie Dough:

- Divide the dough into two equal portions. Flatten each portion into a disk and wrap them in plastic wrap. Chill the dough in the refrigerator for at least 2 hours or until it's firm.

6. Preheat the Oven:

- Preheat your oven to 375°F (190°C). Line baking sheets with parchment paper or silicone baking mats.

7. Roll and Cut Cookies:

- On a lightly floured surface, roll out one of the chilled dough disks to a thickness of about 1/4 inch. Use cookie cutters to cut out shapes.

8. Bake:

- Place the cookies on the prepared baking sheets and bake in the preheated oven for 8-10 minutes or until the edges are lightly golden but the centers are still slightly soft. The exact baking time may vary depending on your oven and the size of your cookies.

9. Cool on a Wire Rack:

- Allow the cookies to cool on the baking sheets for a few min- utes, then transfer them to wire racks to cool completely.

10. Decorate with Royal Icing (Optional):

- If you'd like to decorate your sugar cookies with royal icing, prepare the icing by whisking together powdered sugar, meringue powder, and warm water until it reaches a smooth and glossy consisten- cy. Add food coloring if desired. Use a piping bag or squeeze bottles to decorate your cookies.

11. Enjoy:

- Once the cookies have cooled and the icing has set, enjoy your delicious sugar cookies!

Tips:

- For softer cookies, aim for a shorter baking time, around 8 minutes. For slightly crisper cookies, bake closer to 10 minutes.

- You can use various cookie cutters to create different shapes and sizes of sugar cookies.

- Be creative with your sugar cookie decorations, using col- ored icing, sprinkles, or edible glitter for added flair.

These classic sugar cookies are perfect for holidays, special occasions, or any time you want a sweet treat. Enjoy making and decorating these delightful cookies!

Sheet Pan Chocolate Cake Recipe

Prep Time: 15 minutes | Cook Time: 20-25 minutes | Total Time: 35-40 minutes

Yield: Approximately 12 servings

Ingredients:

For the Cake:

- 2 cups all-purpose flour
- 2 cups granulated sugar
- 1 cup unsweetened cocoa powder
- 2 teaspoons baking powder
- 1 1/2 teaspoons baking soda
- 1 teaspoon salt
- 2 large eggs
- 1 cup buttermilk
- 1 cup strong brewed coffee, cooled
- 1/2 cup vegetable oil
- 2 teaspoons pure vanilla extract

For the Frosting:

- 1 cup (2 sticks) unsalted butter, softened
- 1 cup unsweetened cocoa powder
- 4 cups powdered sugar
- 1/2 cup milk (whole milk or 2% milk)
- 2 teaspoons pure vanilla extract
- Pinch of salt

Instructions:

For the Cake:

1. Preheat the Oven:
- Preheat your oven to 350°F (175°C). Grease and line a 18x13- inch sheet pan with parchment paper, leaving an overhang on the sides for easy removal.
2. Mix Dry Ingredients:
- In a large mixing bowl, whisk together the all-purpose flour, granulated sugar, unsweetened cocoa powder, baking powder, baking soda, and salt until well combined.
3. Combine Wet Ingredients:
- In another bowl, whisk together the eggs, buttermilk, brewed coffee, vegetable oil, and pure vanilla extract.

4. Combine Wet and Dry Ingredients:

· Gradually pour the wet ingredients into the dry ingredient mixture. Stir until the batter is smooth and well incorpo- rated. The batter will be thin; this is normal.

5. Pour into Sheet Pan:

· Pour the cake batter into the prepared sheet pan and spread it out evenly.

6. Bake:

· Bake in the preheated oven for 20-25 minutes, or until a toothpick inserted into the center comes out clean. The exact baking time may vary depending on your oven.

7. Cool:

· Allow the cake to cool in the pan for about 10 minutes, then use the parchment paper overhangs to lift it out of the pan and transfer it to a wire rack to cool completely.

For the Frosting:

1. Make the Chocolate Frosting (or use store bought):

· In a mixing bowl, sift the unsweetened cocoa powder to remove any lumps.

2. In another large mixing bowl, beat the softened butter until creamy. Gradually add the sifted cocoa powder and mix until well combined.

· Add half of the powdered sugar, milk, pure vanilla extract, and a pinch of salt. Beat until smooth. Gradually add the remaining powdered sugar and continue to beat until the frosting is creamy and spreadable. Adjust the consistency with additional milk if needed.

To Assemble:

1. Frost the Cake:

· Once the cake has completely cooled, spread the chocolate frosting evenly over the top.

2. Slice and Serve:

· Slice the sheet pan chocolate cake into squares or rectangles. Serve and enjoy!

Tips:

· You can add chocolate chips, chopped nuts, or chocolate shavings to the cake batter for added texture and flavor.

· Ensure that the coffee is cooled to room temperature before adding it to the batter.

· To make the frosting easier to spread, you can briefly refrigerate it before frosting the cake.

· Store any leftover cake in an airtight container at room temperature or in the refrigerator, depending on your preference.

This sheet pan chocolate cake is a simple and delicious dessert that's perfect for gatherings, potlucks, or when you're craving a classic chocolate cake. Enjoy!

Sheet Pan Vanilla Cake Recipe

Prep Time: 15 minutes | Cook Time: 20-25 minutes | Total Time: 35-40 minutes

Yield: Approximately 12 servings

Ingredients:

For the Cake:

- 2 1/2 cups all-purpose flour
- 2 1/2 teaspoons baking powder
- 1/2 teaspoon baking soda
- 1/2 teaspoon salt
- 1 cup (2 sticks) unsalted butter, softened
- 2 cups granulated sugar
- 4 large eggs
- 2 teaspoons pure vanilla extract
- 1 cup buttermilk

For the Vanilla Buttercream Frosting:

- 1 cup (2 sticks) unsalted butter, softened
- 4 cups powdered sugar
- 1/4 cup milk (whole milk or 2% milk)
- 2 teaspoons pure vanilla extract
- Pinch of salt

Instructions:

For the Cake:

1. Preheat the Oven:
- Preheat your oven to 350°F (175°C). Grease and line an 18x13- inch sheet pan with parchment paper, leaving an overhang on the sides for easy removal.
2. Mix Dry Ingredients:
- In a medium bowl, whisk together the all-purpose flour, baking powder, baking soda, and salt. Set aside.
3. Cream Butter and Sugar:
- In a large mixing bowl, cream together the softened butter and granulated sugar until the mixture is light and fluffy. This should take about 2-3 minutes.

4. Add Eggs and Vanilla:

- Beat in the eggs, one at a time, ensuring each is fully incorporated before adding the next. Mix in the pure vanilla extract.

5. Add Dry Ingredients and Buttermilk:

- Gradually add the dry ingredient mixture to the wet ingredi- ents, alternating with the buttermilk, beginning and ending with the dry ingredients. Mix until just combined, being careful not to over- mix.

6. Pour into Sheet Pan:

- Pour the cake batter into the prepared sheet pan and spread it out evenly.

7. Bake:

- Bake in the preheated oven for 20-25 minutes, or until a toothpick inserted into the center comes out clean. The exact baking time may vary depending on your oven.

8. Cool:

- Allow the cake to cool in the pan for about 10 minutes, then use the parchment paper overhangs to lift it out of the pan and transfer it to a wire rack to cool completely.

-

For the Vanilla Buttercream Frosting (or store bought):

1. Make the Vanilla Buttercream:

- In a mixing bowl, beat the softened butter until creamy.
- Gradually add the powdered sugar, milk, pure vanilla ex- tract, and a pinch of salt. Beat until smoo- th and creamy. Adjust the consistency with additional milk if needed.

To Assemble:

1. Frost the Cake:

- Once the cake has completely cooled, spread the vanilla buttercream frosting evenly over the top.

2. Slice and Serve:

- Slice the sheet pan vanilla cake into squares or rectangles. Serve and enjoy!

Tips:

- You can add food coloring or flavor extracts to the frosting for a customized touch.
- Decorate the cake with sprinkles, chocolate chips, or edible flowers for added flair.
- Store any leftover cake in an airtight container at room temperature or in the refrigerator, depending on your preference.

This sheet pan vanilla cake is a versatile dessert that's perfect for birthdays, celebrations, or anytime you're in the mood for a classic vanilla-flavored treat. Enjoy!

Basic Cupcake Recipe with Flavor Variations

This basic cupcake recipe can be customized with various flavor options. Below, I'll provide the base cupcake recipe followed by several flavor variations.

Base Cupcake Recipe:

Prep Time: 15 minutes | Baking Time: 18-20 minutes | Total Time: 33-35 minutes

Yield: Approximately 12 cupcakes

Ingredients:

- 1 1/3 cups all-purpose or cake flour
- 1 teaspoons baking powder
- 1/4 teaspoon salt
- 1/2 cup (1 stick) unsalted butter, softened
- 1 cup granulated sugar
- 2 large eggs
- 2 teaspoon pure vanilla extract
- 1/2 cup milk

Instructions:

1. Preheat the Oven:
- Preheat your oven to 350°F (175°C). Line a standard muffin tin with paper cupcake liners.
2. Mix Dry Ingredients:
- In a medium bowl, whisk together the all-purpose flour, baking powder, and salt. Set aside.
3. Cream Butter and Sugar:
- In a large mixing bowl, cream together the softened butter and granulated sugar until the mixture is light and fluffy. This should take about 2-3 minutes.
4. Add Eggs and Vanilla:
- Beat in the eggs, one at a time, ensuring each is fully incorporated before adding the next. Mix in the pure vanilla extract.
5. Combine Wet and Dry Ingredients:
- Gradually add the dry ingredient mixture to the wet ingredi- ents, alternating with the milk, beginning and ending with the dry ingredients. Mix until just combined, being careful not to overmix.
6. Fill Cupcake Liners:
7. Spoon or scoop the cupcake batter into the prepared cupcake liners, filling each about 2/3 full.
- Bake:

· Bake in the preheated oven for 18-20 minutes, or until a toothpick inserted into the center of a cupcake comes out clean. The exact baking time may vary depending on your oven.

8. Cool:

· Allow the cupcakes to cool in the muffin tin for a few min- utes, then transfer them to a wire rack to cool completely.

Flavor Variations:

9. Chocolate Cupcakes:

· Add 1/4 cup unsweetened cocoa powder to the dry ingredi- ents for a rich chocolate flavor.

10. Lemon Cupcakes:

· Add the zest of one lemon to the wet ingredients and 2 tablespoons of fresh lemon juice.

11. Strawberry Cupcakes:

· Puree 1/2 cup fresh strawberries and mix them into the wet ingredients.

12. Almond Cupcakes:

· Add 1/2 teaspoon almond extract to the wet ingredients for a delightful almond flavor.

13. Coconut Cupcakes:

· Add 1/2 cup shredded coconut to the batter for a tropical twist.

14. Coffee Cupcakes:

· Dissolve 1 tablespoon of instant coffee granules in the milk before adding it to the batter.

15. Funfetti Cupcakes:

· Fold in colorful sprinkles to the batter for a fun and festive look.

16. Peanut Butter Cupcakes:

· Stir in 1/2 cup creamy peanut butter to the wet ingredients.

Feel free to get creative with your cupcake flavors by mixing and matching different extracts, spices, and add-ins. Once your cup- cakes have cooled, you can frost them with your favorite frosting, such as buttercre- am, cream cheese frosting, or ganache. Enjoy your homemade cupcakes!

Strawberry Shortcake Recipe

Prep Time: 20 minutes | Cook Time: 15 minutes | Chilling Time: 30 minutes | Total Time: 1 hour and 5 minutes

Servings: 6

Ingredients:

For the Shortcakes:

- 2 cups all-purpose flour
- 1/4 cup granulated sugar
- 2 teaspoons baking powder
- 1/2 teaspoon baking soda
- 1/2 teaspoon salt
- 1/2 cup (1 stick) unsalted butter, cold and cubed
- 2/3 cup buttermilk (or milk with 1 tablespoon of lemon juice)
- 1 teaspoon pure vanilla extract
- 1 tablespoon heavy cream (for brushing)

For the Strawberry Filling:

- 4 cups fresh strawberries, hulled and sliced
- 1/4 cup granulated sugar (adjust to taste)
- 1 teaspoon pure vanilla extract

For the Whipped Cream:

- 1 cup heavy whipping cream
- 2 tablespoons powdered sugar
- 1/2 teaspoon pure vanilla extract

Instructions:

For the Shortcakes:

1. Preheat the Oven:
- Preheat your oven to 425°F (220°C). Line a baking sheet with parchment paper.
2. Mix Dry Ingredients:
- In a large mixing bowl, whisk together the all-purpose flour, granulated sugar, baking powder, baking soda, and salt.
3. Cut in Butter:
- Add the cold, cubed butter to the dry ingredients. Use a pastry cutter or your fingers to work the butter into the flour mixture until it resembles coarse crumbs.
4. Add Wet Ingredients:

- Pour in the buttermilk (or milk with lemon juice) and vanilla extract. Stir until the dough just comes together. Do not overmix; it should be slightly shaggy.

5. Form Shortcakes:

- Turn the dough out onto a lightly floured surface and gently knead it a few times to bring it together. Pat the dough into a 1-inch thick rectangle.

- Use a round biscuit cutter (approximately 2.5 to 3 inches in diameter) to cut out shortcakes. Re-roll the scraps and continue cutting until you've used all the dough. You should have about 6 shortcakes.

6. Brush with Cream:

- Place the shortcakes on the prepared baking sheet, leaving some space between each. Brush the tops with heavy cream.

7. Bake:

- Bake in the preheated oven for 12-15 minutes, or until the shortcakes are golden brown. Remove from the oven and let them cool on a wire rack.

For the Strawberry Filling:

1. Prepare Strawberries:

- In a bowl, combine the sliced strawberries, granulated sugar, and vanilla extract. Toss to coat the strawberries evenly. Allow them to macerate for at least 30 minutes at room temperature, or refrigerate if desired.

For the Whipped Cream:

1. Make Whipped Cream:

- In a chilled mixing bowl, whip the heavy whipping cream, powdered sugar, and vanilla extract until stiff peaks form.

2. To Assemble:

- Slice Shortcakes:

- Slice the cooled shortcakes in half horizontally using a serrated knife.

3. Add Strawberries and Cream:

- Spoon a generous amount of macerated strawberries onto the bottom half of each shortcake.

- Top the strawberries with a dollop of whipped cream.

4. Top and Serve:

- Place the top half of each shortcake over the whipped cream, creating a sandwich.

- Optionally, garnish with additional strawberries and a mint leaf.

5. Serve and Enjoy:

- Serve your homemade strawberry shortcakes immediately, and enjoy this classic dessert!

Strawberry shortcake is a delightful treat, especially during the summer months when strawberries are at their peak. Enjoy the combination of sweet, juicy strawberries, fluffy shortcakes, and whipped cream in every bite.

Homemade Apple Pie Recipe

Prep Time: 30 minutes | Cook Time: 50-60 minutes | Total Time: 1 hour 20 minutes

Yield: 1 9-inch pie (8 servings)

Ingredients:

For the Pie Crust:

- 2 1/2 cups all-purpose flour
- 1 teaspoon salt
- 1 teaspoon granulated sugar
- 1 cup (2 sticks) unsalted butter, cold and cubed
- 6-8 tablespoons ice water

For the Apple Filling:

- 6-7 cups of peeled, cored, and thinly sliced apples (about 6-7 medium-sized apples, such as Granny Smith or Honey- crisp)
- 3/4 cup granulated sugar
- 2 tablespoons all-purpose flour
- 1 teaspoon ground cinnamon
- 1/4 teaspoon ground nutmeg (optional)
- 1/4 teaspoon salt
- 1 tablespoon lemon juice
- 1 tablespoon unsalted butter, cut into small pieces

For the Egg Wash:

- 1 egg
- 1 tablespoon water

Instructions:

For the Pie Crust:

1. Mix Dry Ingredients:
- In a large mixing bowl, combine the all-purpose flour, salt, and granulated sugar.
2. Add Cold Butter:

- Add the cold, cubed butter to the flour mixture.

3. Cut in Butter:

- Use a pastry cutter or your fingers to work the butter into the flour mixture until it resembles coarse crumbs with some larger, pea-sized pieces.

4. Add Ice Water:

- Gradually add ice water, one tablespoon at a time, and toss the mixture with a fork until it starts to come together. You may need 6-8 tablespoons of ice water.

5. Form Dough:

- Turn the dough out onto a clean, floured surface. Divide it in half and shape each half into a flat disk. Wrap each disk in plastic wrap and refrigerate for at least 30 minutes.

For the Apple Filling:

1. Prepare Apples:

- Peel, core, and thinly slice the apples. Place them in a large mixing bowl.

2. Add Sugar and Spices:

- In a separate bowl, mix together the granulated sugar, flour, ground cinnamon, ground nutmeg (if using), and salt. Sprinkle this mixture over the sliced apples. Add the lemon juice and toss until the apples are well coated.

To Assemble:

1. Preheat Oven:

- Preheat your oven to 425°F (220°C).

2. Roll Out Pie Crust:

- Roll out one of the chilled pie dough disks on a floured surface to fit a 9-inch pie dish. Place it into the pie dish and trim any excess overhang.

3. Add Apple Filling:

- Fill the pie crust with the prepared apple filling, spreading it out evenly.

4. Dot with Butter:

- Dot the top of the apple filling with small pieces of unsalted butter.

5. Roll Out Second Crust:

- Roll out the second chilled pie dough disk on a floured surface to create the top crust. You can leave it whole or create a lattice or other decorative pattern. If using a whole top crust, make sure to cut a few slits in the center to allow steam to escape.

6. Seal and Brush with Egg Wash:

·   Seal the edges of the top and bottom crusts by crimping them together with your fingers. In a small bowl, whisk together the egg and water to create an egg wash. Brush the top crust with the egg wash.

7. Bake:

·   Place the pie on a baking sheet to catch any drips. Bake in the preheated oven for 50-60 minutes, or until the crust is golden brown and the filling is bubbling. You may need to cover the edges with foil or a pie crust shield to prevent over-browning.

8. Cool and Serve:

·   Allow the apple pie to cool on a wire rack for at least 2 hours before serving. This helps the filling set.

9. Slice and Enjoy:

·   Slice the homemade apple pie and serve it warm or at room temperature. Optionally, serve with a scoop of vanilla ice cream or a dollop of whipped cream.

Enjoy your delicious homemade apple pie with its flaky crust and flavorful apple filling!

Homemade Cherry Pie Recipe

Prep Time: 20 minutes | Cook Time: 45-55 minutes | Total Time: 1 hour 15 minutes to 1 hour 35 minutes

Yield: 1 9-inch pie (approximately 8 servings)

Ingredients:

For the Pie Crust:

- 2 1/2 cups all-purpose flour
- 1 teaspoon salt
- 1 teaspoon granulated sugar
- 1 cup (2 sticks) unsalted butter, cold and cubed
- 6-8 tablespoons ice water

For the Cherry Filling:

- 4 cups fresh or frozen pitted cherries (thawed if using frozen)
- 1 cup granulated sugar (adjust to taste based on cherry sweetness)
- 1/4 cup cornstarch
- 1/4 teaspoon almond extract (optional)
- 1/2 teaspoon vanilla extract
- 1 tablespoon lemon juice
- 1 tablespoon unsalted butter, cut into small pieces

For Assembly:

- 1 egg (for egg wash)
- 1 tablespoon milk or water (for egg wash)
- Extra granulated sugar (for sprinkling on top)

Instructions:

For the Pie Crust:

1. Mix Dry Ingredients:
- In a large mixing bowl, whisk together the all-purpose flour, salt, and granulated sugar.
2. Cut in Butter:
- Add the cold, cubed butter to the flour mixture.
3. Cut the Butter:

- Use a pastry cutter or your fingers to work the butter into the flour mixture until it resembles coarse crumbs with some larger, pea-sized pieces.

4. Add Ice Water:

- Gradually add ice water, one tablespoon at a time, and toss the mixture with a fork until it starts to come together. You may need 6-8 tablespoons of ice water.

5. Form Dough:

- Turn the dough out onto a clean, floured surface. Divide it in half and shape each half into a flat disk. Wrap each disk in plastic wrap and refrigerate for at least 30 minutes.

For the Cherry Filling:

1. Prepare Cherries:

- If using fresh cherries, pit them. If using frozen cherries, make sure they are thawed and well-drained.

2. Mix Filling:

3. In a mixing bowl, combine the pitted cherries, granulated sugar, cornstarch, almond extract (if using), vanilla extract, and lemon juice. Toss until the cherries are evenly coated.

To Assemble:

1. Preheat Oven:

- Preheat your oven to 425°F (220°C).

2. Roll Out Pie Crust:

- Roll out one of the chilled pie dough disks on a floured surface to fit a 9-inch pie dish. Place it into the pie dish and trim any excess overhang.

3. Add Cherry Filling:

- Fill the pie crust with the prepared cherry filling, spreading it out evenly.

4. Dot with Butter:

- Dot the top of the cherry filling with small pieces of unsalted butter.

5. Roll Out Second Crust:

- Roll out the second chilled pie dough disk on a floured surface to create the top crust. You can leave it whole or create a lattice or other decorative pattern. If using a whole top crust, make sure to cut a few slits in the center to allow steam to escape.

6. Seal and Brush with Egg Wash:

- Seal the edges of the top and bottom crusts by crimping them together with your fingers. In a small bowl, whisk together the egg and milk or water to create an egg wash. Brush the top crust with the egg wash.

7. Sprinkle with Sugar:

- Sprinkle the top crust with a little extra granulated sugar for a touch of sweetness and shine.

8. Bake:

- Place the pie on a baking sheet to catch any drips. Bake in the preheated oven for 45-55 minutes, or until the crust is golden brown and the filling is bubbling. You may need to cover the edges with foil or a pie crust shield to prevent over-browning.

9. Cool and Serve:

- Allow the cherry pie to cool on a wire rack for at least 2 hours before serving. This helps the filling set.

10. Slice and Enjoy:

- Slice the homemade cherry pie and serve it warm or at room temperature. Optionally, serve with a scoop of vanilla ice cream for a classic treat.

Enjoy your delicious homemade cherry pie, filled with sweet and juicy cherries, in a flaky, buttery crust!

Easy Eats for Teens has been a delightful journey through the world of simple and delicious recipes designed with teens in mind. We hope this book has not only provided you with easy-to-follow recipes but also inspired your culinary creativity. Remember, cooking is not just about nourishment; it's about the joy of creating something wonderful. We want to extend our heartfelt thanks for choosing our cookbook, and we hope it has brought tasty and memorable moments to your kitchen. Keep exploring, experimenting, and enjoying the art of cooking.

Happy eating!

Made in the USA
Las Vegas, NV
15 December 2024

42aac97d-eec6-410e-b421-1b71e2c616f3R01